Yard and Garden

MAKEOVERS

Your Guide to Creating a Beautiful, Logical Landscape

Yard and Garden MAKEOVERS

Your Guide to Creating a Beautiful, Logical Landscape

George Kay and Brian Kay
With Jennifer Derryberry Mann

Ball Publishing
335 N. River Street
P.O. Box 9
Batavia, IL 60510
www.ballpublishing.com

Library of Congress Cataloging-in-Publication Data

Kay, George, 1929-
  Yard and garden makeovers : your guide to creating a beautiful, logical
landscape / George Kay and Brian Kay with Jennifer Derryberry Mann.
       p. cm.
  Includes index.
  ISBN 978-1-883052-64-5 (hardcover : alk. paper)
  1. Gardens--Design. 2. Landscape design. 3. Landscape architecture. I.
Kay, Brian, 1957- II. Mann, Jennifer Derryberry. III. Title.

  SB472.45.K39 2008
  712'.6--dc22
                                              2007049284

ISBN 978-1-883052-64-5

Printed and bound in Singapore by Imago.
08 09 10 11 12 13 9 8 7 6 5 4 3 2 1

This book is for those who want to create their own beautiful gardens.

There is a logical process to achieving your personal landscape vision. With thoughtful planning, the enjoyment of a warm, welcoming entrance, a wonderful patio setting, and the beauty of plants and nature can be attained by all.

We wish you well on your lifelong relationship with your garden.

Table of Contents

Acknowledgments ix
Introduction xi

PART 1: BEAUTIFUL, LOGICAL DESIGN

1 Simply Beautiful: The Principles of Landscape Design 1
2 Landscape Assessment: Assets and Liabilities 15
3 Entrance and Enclosure: The Front Garden 23
4 Retreat and Recreation: The Back Garden 43
5 Harmony and Style: The Master Plan 67

PART 2: BEAUTIFUL, LOGICAL SELECTIONS

6 Your Landscape Professional: Tips for Working with a Landscape Pro 91
7 Garden Structures: Admire Their Form, Appreciate Their Function 97
8 Beautiful, Logical Plants: Recommendations for Home Landscapes 105

Conclusion 153
About the Authors 155
Index 157

Acknowledgments

We can talk endlessly about landscaping, but staring at a blank sheet of paper has given us a greater respect for writers. Our thanks to Bonnie Riedl, Jason Carlson, Alice Biggers, and Jennifer Derryberry Mann, along with our many landscaping clients and, of course, our families.

Introduction

We, and we are sure you, have poured over beautiful garden books. The illustrations are of marvelous, stately, old gardens and of lovely new gardens that adorn the homes of the famous. Garden envy is never far behind, and it often raises the question, So, what about me? Whether your property is large or small, this book is dedicated to helping you create your own beautiful garden, a garden that you enjoy, that meets your needs and expectations, and that adds beauty to your corner of the world.

Some people would have you believe that architects and "design experts" have mythical powers that allow them to produce great works of art. We disagree. We're inclined to think of the Great and Powerful Wizard of Oz, who, after all the mystery and fanfare, finally took on a more practical approach to helping people. An emphasis on logic and utility is the essence of the design process. With this book we aim to inspire a respect for considering what is logical and what is useful as you set out to beautify your landscape.

Allow us to clear up a landscaping myth right away: Good garden design is not limited to the rich and famous. In fact, no matter what size your property is, the design process is the same. Whether you live in a new cornfield-turned-subdivision or on a property with natural beauty, the design process and design considerations remain constant. In this book we lead you through the design process. We strive to help you become familiar and comfortable with this process so that you will be able to apply it to your own property and create your own beautiful landscape. We can't say it enough: Good design is for everyone.

FORM FOLLOWS FUNCTION

Is there something in your life that works perfectly? Maybe your kitchen is arranged so that it works just right for you. The refrigerator, the stove, the counter space, and the storage—even the kitchen table perfectly stationed in front of the bay window—are all positioned to work in harmony for you. The arrangement is logical, and therefore, it's beautiful.

Landscaping works that way, too. When form follows function, simple elegance often results. Design choices become thoughtful and intentional, rather than stereotypical or trendy. Rather than automatically sticking that ceremonial birch tree 5 ft. from the corner of your house because that's what everyone else has done, consider whether that tree really belongs in that place on *your* property: Why is it placed there? What function or purpose does it serve? Does it look good? Sure, it does now, but what about five years from now, when you will inevitably have to severely prune or remove it before it consumes your house? Is there a more appropriate place for it to be planted? Why not plant it on the perimeter of your property, where it will create dimension, provide privacy, and be allowed to grow to its natural size and beauty? That is, do things because they are appropriate and logical. We will help you answer these questions and more in this book.

It is okay to be critical of landscape design. In fact, we encourage it. By being critical, you will be able to discern the good from the bad, avoid many mistakes, and be on your way to your ideal landscape.

A LANDSCAPE TO LOVE

Drive through many residential neighborhoods these days, and you can't help but notice house after house adorned with a lush, weed-free, carefully mown and watered lawn. But look past all that green grass, and the landscape beyond is often uninspiring. In some cases you'll see a line of overly pruned shrubs clumped beneath window sills, creating a little green "mustache planting." In other cases the lawn has been sodded right up to the foundation, forming a stark edge where house meets earth. In newer neighborhoods it's common to see properties inundated with distracting plants—the latest fads in every size, shape, and color—squeezed up against the house.

Why are such sweeps of green grass, mustache plantings, and faddish plants so common, while truly attractive landscaping is so rare? Caring for grass, although a lot of work, is a familiar and relatively straightforward task for most homeowners. Properly selecting, planting, and caring for trees and shrubs, however, leaves many would-be landscapers feeling confused and overwhelmed. We are afraid of what we don't know. Despite the challenges of landscaping, some homeowners do take it on, usually for one of two reasons: either the trees and shrubs have become such an overgrown tangle that the house is in danger of vanishing from sight, or the homeowners have just built a new home and are dissatisfied with their bleak, sterile yard.

The owner of the newly built home with its new, empty yard may still be recovering from having made thousands of decisions—paint colors, siding materials, electrical outlet covers, floor coverings—and the thought of making a thousand more for the sake of the yard is just too much to take. However, if you are going to spend the time, money, and effort on landscaping your property, isn't it worth it to take the time to do it right? New-construction homeowners have this unique opportunity to create fantastic landscapes that suit their every need and want, because they are starting with a blank canvas. Take advantage of this!

The owner of the older home is presented with an entirely different list of issues. One may be looking for a way out of landscape trouble—quite literally, in fact, if once-popular-plants like the yew or juniper are overgrown and encroaching on the front entrance. The quick fix and easy escape of removing the offending plants leaves another problem: a stark, gaping dead zone at the front door. Another owner is just faced with the boring monotony of Grandma's carefully sculpted yews and yearns for a little excitement in the landscape.

Whether you're facing the never-ending lawn or on the verge of removing every overgrown shrub on your lot, take heart. Good design principles are universal, and good design is for everyone. In the following chapters we outline the principles of landscape design so that you, the homeowner, will be able to make your landscape dreams a reality.

– PART 1 –

Beautiful, Logical Design

1

The Principles of Landscape Design

We each have our own notion of what catches our eye and holds our fancy. But the timeless and the truly beautiful—*that* we tend to agree on: Thomas Jefferson's Monticello, Frank Lloyd Wright's Fallingwater, Michelangelo's Sistine Chapel, and the Leisure Suit. Well, maybe not the leisure suit, but you get the idea. Popular styles come and go; it's the good design principles that are timeless.

The best landscaping design principles are timeless, too. What differentiates good landscaping from the uninspired is functionality, proportion, beauty, and a sense of belonging. Each element in the landscape contributes to a grand sense of harmony, and each element affects the beauty and balance of your garden. The layout and location of each one—patio, walk, wall, sculpture, planter, bench, grill, furniture, play set, pool, gazebo, storage building—must have a meaningful place in your landscape. There's no need to guess or fret about how to accomplish that, though. By following good principles of landscape design, you'll be on your way to creating a beautiful, logical landscape of your own.

PRINCIPLE 1: FOCUS ON FUNCTION

How do you use your yard? What purposes does it serve? The answers to those questions determine how you arrange the hard surfaces and the planting areas in your landscape. As you consider the changes you want to make to your landscape, think about your lifestyle. Do you play with your kids in the backyard? When you walk a visitor to her car, where do you pause for that parting conversation? As you plan your landscape, keep in mind your habits, pastimes, and patterns. Your landscape wish list should be driven by need and function. This is the time-honored essence of design: *Form follows function*. We are more apt to use a well-designed, functional landscape because it is easily accessible and usable. Creating a functional landscape, however, does not require sacrificing beauty. A good landscape is both functional and beautiful.

PRINCIPLE 2: FIRST THE HARDSCAPE

Where will the plants go? That depends on where you locate the walks, patios, and structures, which provide interesting and meaningful areas to plant (fig. 1.1). In fact, designing a functional landscape largely depends on two things: the layout of surfaces

TIP

Walks, patios, and structures set the stage for planting.

Figure 1.1.
By placing the hard surfaces first, you will create areas that frame good planting design.

Figure 1.2.
Trees provide shade, enclosure, comfort, and beauty in the landscape.

and the placement of plants. A good layout of surfaces should be functional and beautiful while also creating pockets of space for plants. That's how you achieve a sense of balance, beauty, and belonging among all elements in your yard and garden.

Depth of field is created through the placement of hard surfaces and plant pockets. It is improved by emphasizing three-dimensional distances. This is done with hedges, walls, street trees, or anything that increases the intensity of depth. Softening hard edges usually means the addition of plants to mute the corners of buildings and the angles in paved surfaces or walls. The improvement in depth and softening of harsh lines adds to the visual experience in the landscape.

PRINCIPLE 3: THEN THE COMPOSITION OF PLANTS

Which plants are most important? Shade trees and large evergreens have the greatest impact on your property. They also take the longest time to mature, so you will want to start with them as early as possible. Start with the big plants, then move on to shrubs, vines, groundcovers, groupings of like plants, and beds of flowers.

Shade trees play a big part in the vibe of a landscape. Next time you drive through a newly developed subdivision, notice the feel of the landscape. The lack of large trees creates a void. Even if the homes are beautiful, the atmosphere is a sterile one without tree cover. Deciduous trees and large evergreens make the greatest impact in your landscape. The beauty of a tree-lined street is only one benefit of these mature plants. The warmth, depth, and comforting feeling of enclosure of a tree-lined street are wonderful (fig. 1.2). And the smaller cooling bill that accompanies a well-shaded property is pretty great, too.

Consider the conundrum in our neighborhood park: When a new jungle gym was built, three shade trees were planted at the northeastern corner of the park. The shade from those trees is a blessing on blistering hot summer afternoons.

TIP

Imagine driving through the woods of a national park. With thoughtful plantings, you can bring a bit of that same beauty and sense of intrigue to your own landscape.

Unfortunately, the shade is nowhere near the jungle gym, which gets so hot on sunny July days that it's unusable. The right trees or shrubs in the right places would make any outdoor space a more comfortable place to be.

PRINCIPLE 4: STRIKE THE RIGHT PROPORTION AND ADD DEPTH

Where will each plant* thrive? Say you buy a 5 ft. wide flowering crabapple to place near the front of your house. This pretty plant can add depth to your landscape and soften the lines of your roof—unless you fall into the common trap of planting it based on its current size. Very simply, that flowering crabapple can grow to be 20 ft. wide. So please, for everyone's sake (including the plant's!), do not place it 4 ft. from the house (fig. 1.5). Otherwise, you'll be forced to endure the pain of butchering its natural beauty in a few short years (fig. 1.4).

Crabapple planting is a frequent and classic example of the rampant poor placement of plants. Honestly, plants really do get bigger, and depending on where in the country you live, they may grow extremely fast. How do you get the right plants in the right place, then? This is one of the most critical questions in planting design, and the

(Clockwise from top left)

Figure 1.3.
This misplaced crabapple was planted too close to the left side of the house. It will require pruning to prevent damage to the home.

Figure 1.4.
The ash shown in this picture has already been subjected to severe pruning due to being planted entirely too close to the house. This makes for an unhappy, and often unattractive, plant.

Figure 1.5.
A tree or shrub placed in the wrong space will require more maintenance and pruning, thus sacrificing its natural beauty.

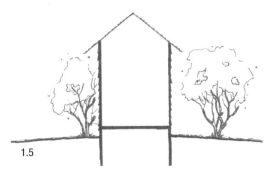

(Top) Figure 1.6.
Don't let its name fool you.
The dwarf burning bush
can grow to be 6–10 ft. tall.

(Bottom) Figure 1.7.
The dwarf Mugo pine
shown here is approxi-
mately 4 ft. tall and 7 ft.
wide, and it can grow
to be 8 ft. tall.

1.6

1.7

TIP

Unless you have an
unlimited budget to
cover the expense of
buying and planting
large trees, you're
probably planting just
a few small trees in
your yard. That may
leave you feeling
ho-hum about your
landscape, but resist
the urge to cluster
trees close together.
Give them adequate
space to grow;
you'll be surprised
how fast they do!

answer—another question—is almost insulting in its simplicity: How big does the plant get? Consider the word "dwarf." The term has created confusion for many people because there's no guarantee that a dwarf in one species is the same size as a dwarf in another. It's all relative between the species and its varieties: a common lilac matures at 12–15 ft., and a dwarf lilac matures at 6–7 ft. (fig. 1.6). It pays to know the difference *before* you put the plant in the ground.

There is no set answer to the nagging question of how far apart to space plants. Make a point to talk with an experienced nurseryman or grower about the plants you're considering planting in your landscape. Or visit a botanical garden, a well-respected landscape architect or designer, or an experienced gardener about the growth habits of your preferred plants. The alternative is that you'll be in for an unpleasant surprise when you discover just how fast and how large your favorite plants grow.

PRINCIPLE 5: CREATE FOCAL POINTS AND ENHANCE VIEWS

What do you see when you look out your windows? If you live on a large property, you may look out on an intriguing woods or an attractive open space. Enhancing such a view may require very few plantings or none at all. Conversely, when you live on a small property with neighbors close at hand, unsightly views can be plentiful. Adding plants to your landscape can create year-round beauty while disguising unsightly views.

Take another look out your windows. You'll notice that the mustache plantings that contractors are fond of planting right next to the house can't be seen at all from inside the house (fig. 1.8). Meanwhile, if you're in a new home, the perimeter of your yard is probably bare. Plant to enhance your view from inside the home, and let that view dictate what passersby see when they look at your yard. Your landscape will look better from every angle.

TIP

If you can't enjoy an outdoor planting from inside your home, you're not making the most of your property. Situate plantings far enough away from the structure of your house that you can see them through your window, typically on the property line.

Figure 1.8. The typical mustache planting, squeezed up against the house, cannot be seen from inside of the house, adds no depth to the property, and makes the home appear small and claustrophobic to passersby.

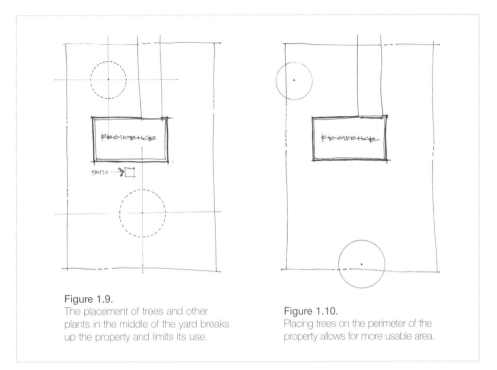

Figure 1.9.
The placement of trees and other plants in the middle of the yard breaks up the property and limits its use.

Figure 1.10.
Placing trees on the perimeter of the property allows for more usable area.

TIP

A big tree in the middle of your front yard visually and physically divides your property into smaller chunks (fig. 1.9). Place the largest trees and evergreens around the perimeter of your property to create the feeling of a comfortably spacious area (fig. 1.10).

PRINCIPLE 6: MATCH THE LANDSCAPE STYLE TO YOUR HOUSE'S ARCHITECTURAL STYLE

Does your home have a distinctive architectural style? If it does, you are very fortunate. Fewer and fewer homes are designed with a strong architectural style, such as Greek Revival, the Classic Farmhouse, Mediterranean, and Victorian, to name a few. If you are one of the lucky few whose home has architectural integrity, you may want to reinforce some of its patterns, shapes, or other details in your landscape's hard surfaces—the walks, the patio, a wall.

With most residential landscaping, the overriding style point is formal vs. informal, or symmetrical vs. asymmetrical. Choosing one style over the other is a decision for you, the homeowner. For instance, if you live in a Cape Cod–style home, you've probably noticed that its design is symmetrical. That's mostly the case with Cape Cods: the front door is in the middle, and there are an equal number of windows on both sides of it. Although the Cape Cod's symmetry lends itself to a formal landscape (fig. 1.11A), this style of home is often considered ideal for an informal cottage garden (fig. 1.11B). Either choice—formal landscaping or informal—is a good one if it follows good design principles and pleases your eye.

Figure 1.11.
These two plans show the same Cape Cod house designed in a formal (A) and informal (B) style. Choosing the style of your landscape is one of personal taste. A garden can be designed as either formal or informal, and still be considered classic. Remember, choose a style that will best fit your needs and serve your functions.

TIP

Most builders who cater to the masses look for ways to keep costs down. That generally means minimizing a home's unique details. This often results in monotony and ultimately leads to cookie-cutter homes and landscaping.

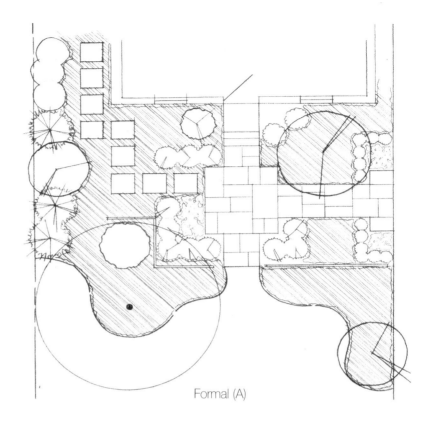

Formal (A)

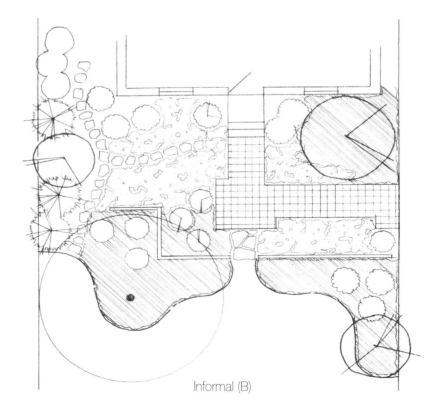

Informal (B)

(Clockwise from top)

Figure 1.12.
A Statue of Liberty replica makes a huge impact in the front yard, but it's not a good one! Sometimes less is more. Remember, not everyone shares your personal taste.

Figure 1.13.
The thoughtful placement of statuary among plants creates a sense of belonging that is pleasing to view in the back garden.

Figure 1.14.
Statuary is a matter of personal taste. Avoid placing doodads and other distracting knick-knacks in the front yard.

Figure 1.15.
Art pieces such as these are beautiful nestled in the backyard landscape.

TIP

Keep the front yard free from the distraction of elaborate garden design and yard art. As the saying goes, don't put ten pounds of doodads in a five-pound bag!

PRINCIPLE 7: BE A GOOD NEIGHBOR

When you drive past your home at 30 miles per hour, what do you see? The intricate details of a garden cannot be appreciated when driving by in a car. Still, the common tendency is to do too much landscaping in the front yard.

Just about everyone has an example like this: In our town there's a front yard that boasts a 6 ft. replica of the Statue of Liberty, a supporting cast of two smaller statues, a gazing ball, two benches (unmatched, of course), and a mural painted on the wood gates leading to the backyard. Why have they done this? Who knows? But I shudder to think what's inside the house!

While we strive to avoid monotony in design, adding whimsical figurines to the front yard is not the way to distinguish yourself. The front yard benefits from simplicity, because the main goal is to direct visitors to the front door. Distractions add nothing to the visual experience of spotting the front door, nor do they improve the view of it.

1.16

Privacy plantings perform an important function. Make them attractive so they do their job in a subtle and interesting way, rather than send an overt "Keep out!" message.

1.17

Figures 1.16 and 1.17.
A good plant screen should not only provide privacy but also look natural and beautiful. Notice in these pictures how the planting screens both the road and the neighbor's property.

If you feel compelled to display garden art, the logical location is the backyard, where you can share your self-expression with family and houseguests rather than the general public. The backyard is also an environment better suited for appreciating your garden art. You're more apt to be sitting in the backyard, so you're better able to see and enjoy more intricate design details, such as statuary and individual flowers. The backyard also provides more planting backdrops to highlight your art and flowers.

TIP

Good planning sets the stage for long-term improvement and accommodates the many unforeseen changes your life will bring.

PRINCIPLE 8: MAINTAIN PRIVACY

How much privacy do you want your landscaping to provide? The need for privacy is unique to each person, and feelings about it range from "I like being able to see the cars go by" to "I don't want to talk to my neighbor every time I go outside." Planting along the property line can make you feel comfortable in your own setting, both by providing privacy and by screening objectionable views.

PRINCIPLE 9: AVOID MISTAKES

Will my landscaping plan stand the test of time and years of change? Careful examination of all the design elements you plan to include in your personal landscape will help you avoid mistakes. Seldom do good results occur when you rush the process. Take your time in developing a carefully considered plan. Unlike the construction of a home, the landscaping plan and the landscaping itself can gradually be developed through the years—even over the entirety of the time you live in your home.

PUT THE PRINCIPLES TO WORK

Good design principles are timeless. By following them, you'll have a yard that works well with your life, and you'll create beauty and balance that grow with your ever-changing landscape. With trees, shrubs, and other plants placed properly in relation to the hardscape, an adaptable sense of proportion and depth will emerge. And as your plants mature over time, beautiful focal points and strong sight lines will create views that highlight your home's architectural character or your own personal sense of style.

This book will help you avoid landscaping mistakes. The first step in achieving landscaping perfection is to minimize the things that can go wrong. In the next few chapters, we'll show you examples of properties that suffered from misguided hardscapes and unfortunate plantings—and how good design principles transformed these yards into simple, beautiful landscapes. From those examples you'll be prepared to analyze your goals objectively, develop a plan, and create a garden that gets better with time.

CHAPTER 2

Landscape

Assets and Liabilities

Good design principles make for more beautiful and more functional landscapes. To apply those principles to your property, you must first assess the assets and liabilities in your yard and garden. Approach the task like a pro, trying to see your house with fresh eyes: Park on the street a good distance from your home and, approaching your property on foot, review its conditions and characteristics and take note of all you see. For a moment set aside the opinions—good and bad—you already hold about your existing landscape. Be as objective and critical as possible of your property and the views of the surrounding neighborhood.

This level of objectivity is vital to making honest assessments. Walk around your entire property, analyzing both its good and its undesirable facets. Additionally, go inside and look out each of your windows and ask the question, What do I see? This exercise will help you answer the more interesting question, What do I *want* to see?

PLAT OF SURVEY

When you bought your home, one of the documents present at closing was the plat of survey (fig. 2.1). The plat indicates the location of the permanent structures on your property: the house, garage, driveway, front walk, and so on. To better work with the plat of survey, enlarge it to a scale such as 1 in. = 8 or 1 in. = 10 ft. With this enlarged document, you'll be able to locate and mark additional existing elements, such as the following, accurately (fig. 2.2):

STRUCTURES	LANDSCAPING AND RECREATION
Windows	Plants
Deck	Vegetable garden
Patio	Statues
Pergola	Swing set
Swimming pool	Sandbox
Fences	Grill
Paths	Basketball hoop
Utility boxes	Soccer net
Telephone poles	Baseball backstop

After summarizing the details of your property on the plat of survey, sketch the off-site views—your neighbors' properties. Eyeballing and estimating is the way to go here, since using a tape measure might cause some controversy. When you survey your neighbors' properties, you're looking for the same elements that you've identified on your property, though in their cases, you need only to be concerned with the elements that affect your home and your view.

Glaringly unattractive off-site views may include swing sets, campers, cars on blocks, unscreened storage areas, and the like. These are the kinds of sights that prompt privacy screening (fig. 2.3). If, however, you have beautiful off-site views, such as of a park, or you enjoy your neighbor's perennial garden, then you are truly fortunate. Not to be forgotten during your assessment are off-site trees that have an influence on your property: nearby trees may provide shade or create a wonderful scene, or they may be a nuisance because they drop branches or berries on your property. While conducting your landscape assessment, the goals are to identify all your views and to decide which ones you'd like to change.

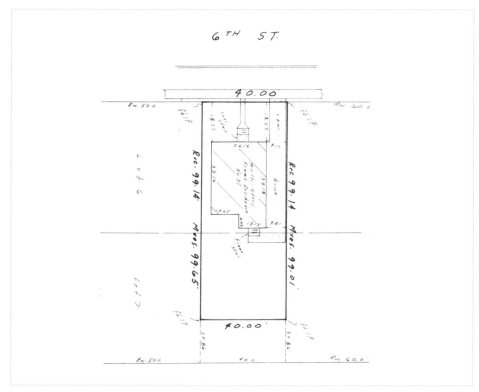

TIP

As you take stock of all aspects of your property and draw them in on your plat of survey, you may be amused by the number of items in your yard.

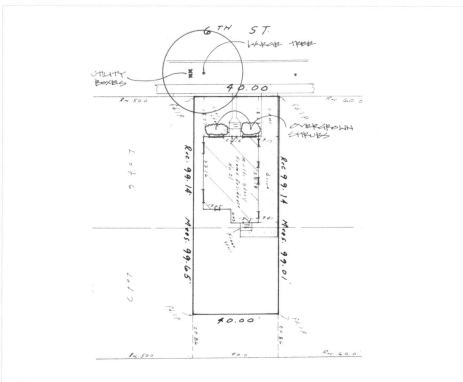

Figure 2.2.
As you assess your property, make note of major existing elements—such as shrubs, trees, and swing sets—that may influence your landscape design.

Figure 2.3.
Paying close attention to the off-site elements that affect your property—such as houses, sheds, parking lots, swing sets, cars, and many more—is important when deciding what areas you want to screen from your view.

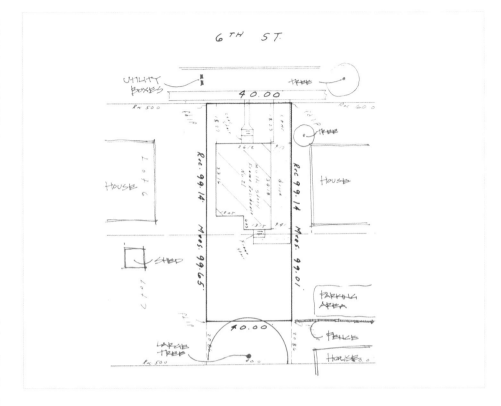

Take a tip from farmers: They often plant evergreen screens on the west and north sides of their fields to create windbreaks (fig. 2.4).

(Left to right)

Figure 2.4.
The windbreak in this plan is more typical on an older farm. The double row of evergreens provides a good barrier from the prevailing north and west winds.

Figure 2.5.
The more natural appearance of this windbreak is accomplished by using a variety of plants.

Figure 2.6.
Notice where your property has shade or needs shade at every hour of the day.

ORIENTATION

Whether your home is positioned north to south or east to west, its orientation is sure to affect your experience living there. You may love sitting in your kitchen drinking coffee in the morning part of the year, for instance, but find that the sunrise blinds you the rest of the time. Or a predominant wind may force you to avoid your front door at certain times of the year. Remedies for such sun and wind issues not only improve the obvious problems but also may reduce utility usage and expense.

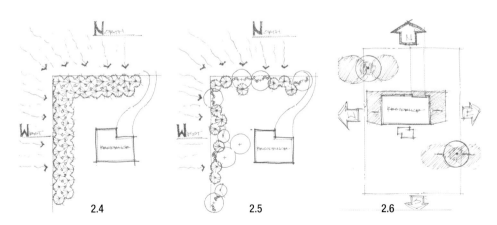

2.4   2.5   2.6

DRAINAGE

Perhaps one of the most important but overlooked issues on your property is drainage. During the home inspection that took place (or should have taken place) when you bought your home, your inspector should have revealed any areas with questionable drainage. A common problem is settling around the foundation that causes water to drain toward the house (fig. 2.7). Another one is a sump pump that doesn't empty out and away from the house, instead acting like a recirculation pump. It's also possible that your property is the low point on your block, meaning several other houses drain toward yours. None of these problems sentences you to a landscape full of water headaches, but as a precaution, you'll want to maintain positive drainage—that is, drainage that goes away from your home (fig. 2.8).

Although the more important thing, of course, is keeping your house dry, keep an eye on your plants, too: some do better in wet areas than others. One symptom of poor

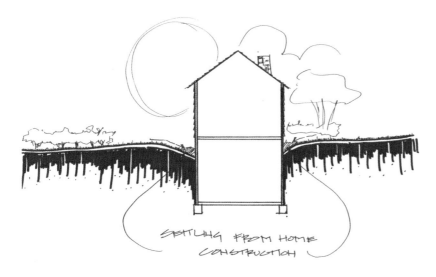

Figure 2.7.
Settling around the foundation of your home can cause some serious grading issues. With the ground sloping toward the home, water pools around the foundation and can leak into the basement. Noticing grading issues is an important step to take at the beginning of the landscape design phase.

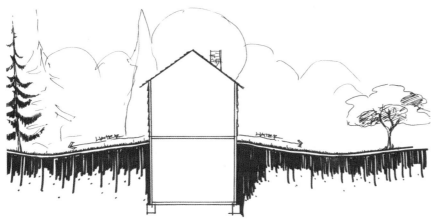

Figure 2.8.
Correcting grading issues can be as easy as sloping the ground away from the house.

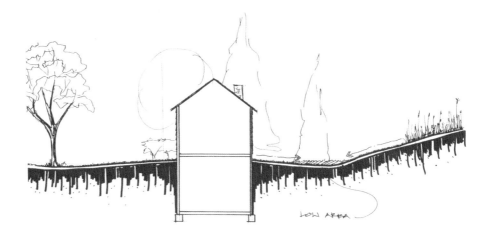

landscape drainage may be an area that stays damp most of the time. It could be that the area is flat, stays shaded, or is part of a swale that is just slow to drain. If you are unable to improve drainage in these areas, then your plant selection should focus on plants that tolerate and even thrive in wet locations.

CURRENT FUNCTIONS

During your assessment, ask, Is the patio large enough for my family reunion? Do I have enough room in the backyard to play baseball? Develop a list of features that are relevant to you and your family. Whatever is important to you and whatever you are considering doing on your property, now is the time to evaluate what elements your property has and what you can add. For instance, a baseball diamond may not be possible, but with a couple small changes to the backyard, you could have plenty of room to play catch.

Following is an example of the kind of list you might create. Start by writing down the big categories, such as what you like about your property, what you dislike, and what you'd like to add. Then think on all your property's features and brainstorm positive and negative issues with them and jot them down in the appropriate categories.

What I like about my property
Size allows me to play sports.
Afternoon shade where I spend time outside after work.
The slope because my children love to sled.
The surrounding woods are beautiful and full of wildlife.
The sun allows me to have a colorful perennial garden.
There's a beautiful stream in the back.
I back up to a quiet park.
This small space is all I need.

What I dislike about my property	*What I'd like to add to my space*
Neighbors are too close.	Large patio
I'm tired of looking at my neighbor's swing set.	Big lawn area
I have a tree in the middle of the yard, so I can't set up any games for the children.	Pool or spa
	Area for wildlife
It's too sunny in the back.	Pond
It's too shady in the front.	Basketball court
There's too much maintenance.	Extra parking
I don't have room for a pool.	Privacy

Once you've made this assessment, you can start the tough work of prioritizing the items! Keeping in mind the preservation or enhancement of the property features you already like, think of solutions to the problems and of the specific places where you could add items from your wish list.

TAKING STOCK

A thorough landscape assessment is the key to a good landscape design. Don't skip or skimp on this phase. Remember, your landscape is an investment. It will require time, thought, and effort. And when it's developed with thoughtfulness and care, you will see your masterpiece unfold before your eyes.

Entrance and

The Front Garden

Imagine yourself a guest visiting your house for the first time. When you drive up to it, what do you see? Can you easily find the sidewalk and quickly locate the front door? Does the yard seem inviting? Is the landscape design logical? Or is your eye drawn to the dreaded concrete goose with the festive scarf?

A truly welcoming entrance to your home should offer a clear sight line to the front door, a wide walkway from the street, and plenty of room to maneuver along the way—with no distractions. After all, one of the most important purposes of your front yard is to welcome people to your home. Your landscape shouldn't make them question your taste.

Of equal importance is providing a sense of enclosure from the outside world. This gives your home and your property a tranquil environment. Good landscape design will create visual interest from inside the house and out, enhance privacy, and screen unattractive views. Of course, this consideration is particularly important if your next-door neighbor keeps an RV the size of Montana.

Unfortunately, for many homes the front yard does not fulfill its essential purposes of welcome and enclosure. Instead, many front entrances try too hard to impress. The clutter of trendy but distracting plants and doodads can make finding the entrance a challenge. On the other extreme, the front yard may take the form of the barren suburban wasteland often seen in new, treeless developments: A solitary stick of a tree and a few small shrubs dot the landscape, while a giant driveway serves as a walkway that narrows into a small sidewalk that completes the path to the front door. The result is that the visitor's eye is drawn straight to the three-car garage.

The solution to creating a welcoming ambience, entrance, and sense of enclosure is to create a landscape plan for the front walk and the surrounding plantings. That plan should complement the front entrance and the architecture of the home to create a sense of comfort and serenity.

TIP

Cookie-cutter plans just don't cut it.

PLAN YOUR FRONT LANDSCAPE

- First design the entire front-entrance garden. In this design include a beautifully functional and friendly front walk, taking care with its placement, size (4 ft. width minimum), and materials.
- Create beautiful views that can be enjoyed from inside the home and out.
- Ensure your privacy with trees, shrubs, evergreens, and walls or fences.
- Plan a balanced composition of trees, shrubs, evergreens, flowers, and lawn.
- Consider how much maintenance your plantings will require—and whether you have the time or resources to do that maintenance.
- Install the hardscape elements, including sidewalks and retaining walls, before the plants.

THE HARDSCAPE

The place to start in designing your front yard is the *hardscape*, relatively permanent structural elements—such as the driveway, sidewalks, fences, and retaining walls—which form the foundation of your landscape design. Why start here? Heavy construction and grading may be involved, and you don't want to waste time and money planting something that could be damaged during future construction.

Grading. Before starting any hardscape construction, ensure that your front yard is graded properly to allow for effective drainage. Even if you have to start over and regrade the entire yard, do it. Your work improving drainage will be rewarded by keeping your plants healthy, your basement dry, and your yard free of post-rainstorm lakes. The *soil grade*, or ground level, should be highest at the house and gradually move lower to the perimeter of your property. If it doesn't, you'll have problems. Unless you own a tractor or a Bobcat, you'll probably need to hire a professional for this work, since heavy equipment is typically involved.

Retaining wall. If your property slopes to the street so much that you lack ample level space for a proper front walk and a planting pocket or two to help soften the lines of your home, consider adding a retaining wall. The minimum height for a retaining wall is 15 in. Anything lower than that ends up looking like stone edging rather than a wall. We also recommend that you build a continuous wall—rather than installing a collection of random rocks, a mistake that many landscape companies let their customers make, probably because installing a few stones is easier work than building a wall. A retaining wall will resolve your grading issues by lessening the slope and creating a more level area for the front walk and entrance garden.

Stones scattered around a property distract and interrupt the view and create the haphazard appearance of a stone quarry. A retaining wall, on the other hand, provides interest and depth. We heartily endorse using real stone for the wall. The concrete block so prevalent in home landscapes today is much too reminiscent of department of transportation projects, gas stations, and—dare we say it—prisons.

Figure 3.1.
This low retaining wall (approx. 18 in.) adds depth and provides a level area for the front walk.

Fences. Fencing can be used for multiple purposes, including privacy, security, decoration, noise reduction, and space definition. A fence can outline the entire property or define specific areas, such as the entrance or a flower garden.

Figure 3.2.
This picket fence adds
depth and a visual separation between the public
walk and the front garden.

Fencing materials and design should complement the home's architecture. Fence types include split rail, picket, slat (solid board), lattice, basket weave, board and batten, and decorative wrought iron. We do not recommend chain-link fencing, unless you want your garden to look like a little league field.

How much is enough? In almost every case, you should avoid fences that will block out all views. Wide-board vertical wooden fences are too overwhelming for most residential landscapes. Split rail, picket, and wrought iron fences can create borders for your property while still allowing for plenty of air circulation and visibility.

The main purpose of a fence is to provide some sort of separation. This purpose, however, can also be achieved by using a simple composition of plants to form a hedge or screen. Consider using fencing materials in concert with plant materials for privacy and property definition.

Driveway and garage door

The driveway usually starts at the front of the home, from the street, even if it ends in the back, so it's an important part of the front yard.

We suggest that you avoid the circular drive, which often doubles as a parking area. Unless you live on an estate-sized property, a circular drive really doesn't work all that well from an aesthetic standpoint. A circular drive would dominate the typical suburban landscape, with too much pavement and too little room for planting. If you need extra parking, you can create a parking area off the main drive or near the street, if space permits, where the expanse of hard surface will be less obtrusive.

An important principle in landscape design is to highlight your house, rather than your driveway or your garage. Lining the drive with runway lights or hostas, one or more of which are bound to be run over, only highlight the driveway, which is a purely functional element. Good driveway design is subdued, using materials with dark colors, which fade into the background.

An unfortunate amount of suburban architecture seems focused on the garage door. "Side-loading" garages are ideal for hiding garage doors from the eyes of approaching visitors. But too many homes have three or four garage doors in prominent view right in front, as if you own a garage with an attached house. If that sounds like your home, don't despair. You can minimize your garage doors by simplifying the design elements and painting the doors to virtually disappear. Eliminate intricate designs (especially murals), fancy windows, or wood patterns that draw the eye. We once saw garage doors labeled "his" and "hers." We wish we hadn't. Such self-expression out in the open is neither cute nor endearing—and at its worst, it distracts drivers who should have their eyes on your neighborhood street.

Figures 3.3 and 3.4.
Both of these front walks wind through plantings that create interest and beauty on the way to the front door.

A friendly front walk

One of the biggest culprits in poor landscape design is the front walk. In almost every case, landscape design can be greatly improved by replacing the standard walkway.

If you are building a new home, ask the contractor to refrain from putting in the typical "builder's walk." It's often too narrow, too short, and too close to the house to allow for a pleasing layout of trees, shrubs, and plants. Instead, develop a design for the front walk that incorporates logical principles of placement, size, and materials—or hire a landscape architect to create and implement a landscape plan with a proper walk.

Placement. Ideally, the front walk should extend to the area where guests will park, whether on the street, in a private parking area, or on the driveway on your property. If the walk must stem from the driveway, allow plenty of space between the walk and the house—at least 12 feet—for plantings. That depth allows for more flexibility in the use of plant material, which can help you soften the lines of the house and ensure a beautiful view from indoors.

When designing your walk, plan for angles. Changing directions in 90-degree angles, rather than with a curve, creates a stronger architectural element. A good rule of thumb is that a sidewalk shouldn't curve unless it has to curve around something that's already there, such as a tree. Even then, it would be better to angle around it, if space permits.

Size. The standard builder's front "cattle walk" is 3 ft. wide, which is too narrow to make you and your guests feel comfortable standing or walking side by side. A minimum width of 4 ft. is required to accommodate two people walking together. The best walks also include a larger area where you can stop and talk with your guests as they are coming and going. Consider creating a larger terrace or surface near the front door or farther down the walk to accommodate gatherings of two or more people. These larger areas give more strength and scale to the front walk than a straight line.

Materials. The materials you use in your front walk should enhance your landscape design and complement your home. Consider the architectural style and colors of your home when selecting the material for your front walk. Avoid competing colors.

Clay brick pavers, bluestone, and other natural stones are timeless, classic choices for walks, although they are more expensive than concrete or concrete pavers. The stones may be either irregular or cut to specifications. Using different materials for different areas of the walk adds interest and dimension.

There's nothing wrong with using concrete, though. Concrete is the least expensive choice, requires little maintenance, and, for the lucky, lasts as long as thirty years. You can give concrete greater appeal by defining sections and adding a brushed surface. Stamped and colored concrete is too busy for an elegant landscape.

The design of the walk is the most important element, although function is also critical. Remember your guests' comfort. Make sure that a lady wearing high heels will be able to navigate the front walk gracefully, even if most of your foot traffic is kids in sneakers.

THE PLANTINGS

The most prominent feature of most residential landscapes is the lawn, but with all that grass come chemicals and maintenance. Herbaceous and woody plantings have their own maintenance needs, too, but these are often less time-consuming than grass's. As you are considering the different elements of your landscape, be sure to think about the maintenance requirements.

Grass takes up more than its fair share of the average landscape because it's not intimidating; its maintenance requirements are straightforward. But even though mowing doesn't require much skill, it certainly requires a great deal of time. Do you have the time to take care of the lawn yourself, or will you need to hire a maintenance company? How much lawn is enough for the front? (Keep in mind that the front lawn is not really intended as an athletic field.)

If you have shady areas from trees, consider using shade-tolerant groundcover instead of grass. Many forms of groundcover are virtually maintenance free, once established. The transition from taller plants to groundcover also brings the benefit of softening and unifying the landscape. For sunnier spots, consider sun-tolerant groundcover instead of grass.

Research the habits of plants before you buy them. Some of the more popular shrubs require a great deal of maintenance to retain their shape and smaller size. That's also true of hedges that need pruning. You may like the look of the straight lines of a formal boxwood hedge, but remember that it requires trimming at least once a year. (This is still less maintenance than caring for grass!)

Flowers, both annual and perennial, require a lot of maintenance. All flowers require watering during dry spells. Container gardens are even higher maintenance, requiring watering on a daily basis during the dog days of summer. Perennials will spread and require splitting every few years. Also, remember that flowers are visible in the landscape for only a few months out of the year. Avoiding large areas of flowers will eliminate unsightly voids in your landscape during the winter months. If you like flower color, but want to minimize the accompanying work, plant flowers in small areas near the home, such as at the front entrance or around a patio. This allows easy access for watering, eliminates dragging the hose through the yard, and makes maintenance much simpler. A good rule of thumb: the farther away you plant flowers from the house, the harder and more time consuming it is to care for them.

If you enjoy working in the garden, the sky's the limit with your landscape plan. If you just don't have the time or the inclination, plan your landscape according to your maintenance abilities.

Plan the right composition

Good landscape design is a pleasing composition of a variety of plant materials, but it's best to start planning at the top—with the trees. Shade trees are the stalwarts of any property. Trees have the greatest impact on the landscape, creating the backdrop for all other elements and offering screening, noise reduction, shade, and many other comforts.

Consider the following questions. Do you have existing trees? If so, do you want to keep them all, or should some be removed? Determine whether each tree is a nuisance or a treasure.

Do you need to plant trees to provide shade or a windbreak or to screen objectionable views? Plan for the future when selecting deciduous trees and evergreens, which may mean ten to twenty years down the road before the tree reaches its full maturity. You can plant small trees, but remember that they will grow to be just as big as the tag says. So you don't lose valuable growing time, get your major trees in the ground quickly, as soon as you're certain of their placement and species. Then consider the impact of those magnificent shade trees on your future shrubs and flowers and plan accordingly.

Create beautiful views. In planning for trees and shrubs, imagine them not only as they will look outside but also what views they'll create when seen from inside the house. Too often, inexperienced gardeners will plant a 2 ft. shrub in front of a window, only to have it grow to cover up the entire view in a few years. Consider the location when you make your plant selection based on its size and habit, such as multiple stems and ascending branches. If you want to have a flowering tree, for example, as part of your view from indoors, place it 10–15 ft. away from the window, where it can be seen but won't block the view.

Most woody plants can be pruned, of course, to fit in a too-small space, but you may remove the beauty of upcoming flowers and stunt the plant's natural growth. Pruning should be done judiciously, after determining the best way to prune each particular species.

Improve the views. Good landscape planning creates beauty and comfort by changing the views, from inside and out, that are not pleasing. The view from the front entrance garden typically includes the public sidewalk, the street, and garages across the street and next door. Depending on your neighbor's activities and habits, you may also see a basketball hoop, aging cars, or a collection of garbage cans. Screening such objectionable views is an important goal of a good landscape plan.

The right landscape design will keep the eye drawn to the entrance of your home and the area around it, rather than to the perimeter of the property and your neighbors' lackluster choices.

FRONT GARDEN MAKEOVER
WELCOME HOME: THE SCHIFFER HOUSE

3.5

3.6

The Schiffers decided to make over their new front yard, after having recently moved from Chicago to a country setting about 40 miles northwest of the city. The Schiffers were eager to escape the hustle and bustle of the city, and they were excited to welcome friends and family to their wooded retreat. But a steep grade change in the front yard gave the house a "high on a hill" feeling of isolation. To overcome that, the Schiffers wanted an entrance garden that would warmly welcome their visitors, while giving their home a connection to the surrounding woods.

Driveway. The drive leading to the Schiffer house meanders through the woods, creating a dramatic approach. It was decided to construct a stone retaining wall to frame the front entrance and to help flatten the steep grade that marred the front yard.

Front walk. Between the wall and the house, a 4-foot-wide bluestone walk was installed to lead guests from the drive to the door. The design of the walk is quite simple—no dramatic meandering here—and a small, expanded area created a space for

TIP

Your front walk should be at least 4 ft. wide. That's enough space for two people to walk side by side, but not so big that it overwhelms your front yard.

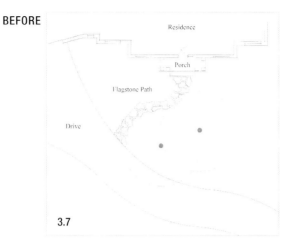

3.7

Residence

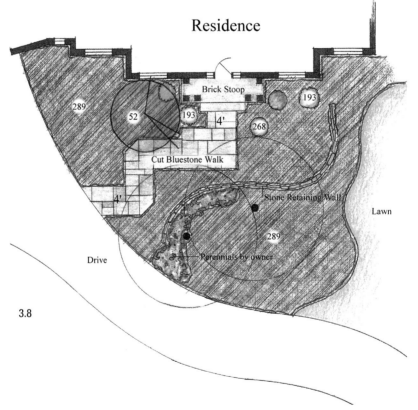

3.8

a few guests to congregate and visit as they arrive and depart. Don't be fooled by the simplicity of the design: this kind of front walk is highly effective in drawing people into your home and making them feel comfortable.

Another comfort measure along the walk comes from the surrounding planting, which softens the hard surfaces. The walk was placed about 25 ft. from the face of the garage to create enough space for a plant of significant size and interest. The Schiffers have a serviceberry, which boasts clusters of white flowers and dark purple berries and can grow to about 15 ft. tall. A plant of this size helps scale down the house and soften the corners of the house and its roofline.

Plants. The Schiffers don't exactly have green thumbs, but they still wanted a lush, attractive garden—with minimal maintenance. A simple planting scheme was the answer. To keep the maintenance requirements on the low side, only four varieties of plants are included in the front yard, and there are only a few areas for flowers, which require the most maintenance.

So how is this lush garden setting achieved? Groundcover! With many varieties to choose from, groundcover is a simple and effective way to unify your garden. The Schiffers' groundcover is evergreen, giving the garden a flourishing look year-round. Groundcover also adds another layer of dimension beneath the woody plants in the garden. Once a groundcover is established—in two to three years, with proper care—it is low maintenance, it ties everything together, and it greatly reduces the need for numerous plants and flowers, yet drawing attention to the flowers you do include in the garden.

Why it works. This front yard is elegant, simple, welcoming, and lush, while coordinating beautifully with its surrounding woods. The success of this design can be measured by its year-round appeal and minimal maintenance needs.

3.9

Figure 3.9.
A stone retaining wall flows through the new landscape and blends in with the woods, connecting the house with its surroundings.
A simple planting scheme creates a lush garden that requires little maintenance. The Schiffers' front yard has only four varieties of plants, with a low-maintenance evergreen groundcover as the garden mainstay. And there are only a few areas dedicated to flowers, which require the most attention.

2

CURB APPEAL: THE POWERS HOUSE

3.10

3.11

3.12

This house in the western suburbs of Chicago prominently featured the most common contractor flaws: a single-file cattle walk leading to the front door, minimal and uninspired landscaping, and no privacy whatsoever. As a real estate agent, the owner knew very well the importance of curb appeal. Add to that his interest in gardening and landscaping, and it was a simple decision to replace the original cookie-cutter landscape with a proper front entrance garden.

A spacious walkway. The contractor's standard 3 ft. wide walk was removed and replaced with a 4 ft. wide walk leading to the front door. An extra foot may not seem like much—and in terms of materials and expense, it's not—but it makes a world of difference in welcoming you and your guests into your home with a sense of comfort and thoughtfulness. The wider walk allows two people to walk side by side. A small expanded area at the corner of the walk allows the homeowners to meet, greet, and bid farewell to visitors without having to stand in the driveway or lawn.

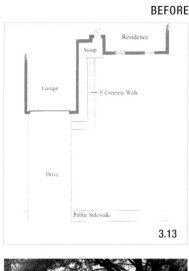

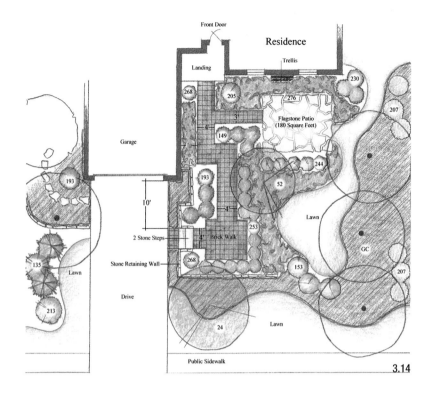

Figure labels in plan (3.14): Front Door, Residence, Trellis, Landing, 230, 268, 205, 276, 207, Flagstone Patio (180 Square Feet), Garage, 149, 193, 52, 244, 10', 193, 2 Stone Steps, 4" Brick Walk, 253, Stone Retaining Wall, 268, 135, Lawn, 213, Drive, 153, 207, GC, Lawn, 24, Lawn, Public Sidewalk, 3.14

Figure labels in plan (3.13): Residence, Stoop, Garage, 3' Concrete Walk, Drive, Public Sidewalk, 3.13

3.15

Figure 3.15.
This small flagstone surface in the front yard provides a place to sit and—with a privacy planting—a sense of intimacy.

Front porch. Another frequent flaw in many newer suburban homes is the lack of a front porch. The Powerses added a small flagstone patio with a seating area that functions much like the traditional front porch. Here they can sit, relax, and take in the sights and sounds of the neighborhood.

Retaining wall. To frame the front entrance garden, accommodate a 24 in. grade change, and add depth as viewed from the street, a low retaining wall was added. The design of the wall allowed a garden to be developed around the walk and patio, creating a very welcoming and intimate front entrance.

Plants for privacy and a pleasant space. Strategically placed plants around the patio accomplished two things. In terms of function, they created a screen from the road, which gave the house some privacy. Considering form, the plants improved the view of the property, both for the Powerses, as they looked out over their garden from the patio, and for neighbors driving by. The result is a comfortable and enjoyable front yard.

A room outdoors. The owners are now comfortable outside and find themselves actively involved in caring for their property. While the landscaping work was being done, the Powerses also took care to learn about the proper methods of pruning and landscape maintenance—although with the plants placed in ideal locations throughout this landscape, they won't require much in terms of extra care.

CAPE COD STYLE: THE SCHULENBURG HOUSE

3.16

3.17

When the Schulenburgs moved into their 1950s-era Cape Cod–inspired home, they loved the simple, pleasing architecture, but the existing landscape lacked similar good looks. An expanse of lawn stretched from the public sidewalk all the way to the house, making the property look sterile. The challenge was to design an entrance garden that would highlight the distinct architecture, create a courtyardlike setting, and provide a sense of enclosure and privacy.

Beautifully fenced in. Because the front yard sloped toward the street, a stone retaining wall was built out near the public sidewalk to create a level, larger space for the front entrance area. Then, 4 ft. inside the wall, a charming picket fence was constructed to complement the home's architecture. Even at only 42 in. tall, this open, airy fence adds a comforting sense of enclosure for the area (fig. 3.3). Given that the driveway runs right along the property line on this very narrow lot—eliminating any chance of adding a privacy planting—the element of enclosure around the front entrance courtyard is all the more important.

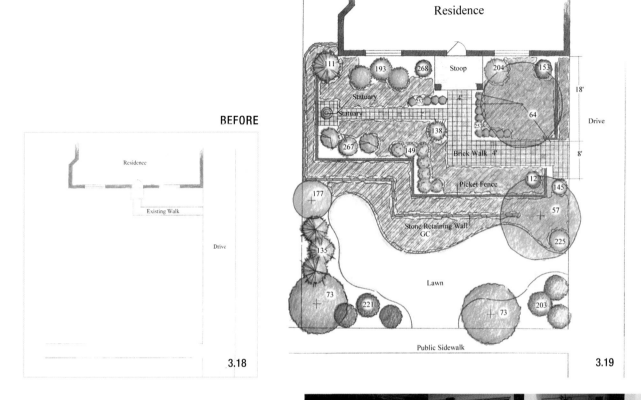

BEFORE

3.18

3.19

Front walk. A very simple brick surface that measures 4-foot-wide (again, large enough for two people!), the front walk leads from the drive to the front entrance. Unlike the typical builder walk, which tends to be a mere 3–4 ft. from the house, the walk is 18 ft. away, making room for a meaningful planting between the walk and the house. The planting not only adds interest as you approach the front entrance, but it also softens the hard surfaces to make the area look much more full and lush.

Plantings with purpose. The homeowners, being avid gardeners, wanted many areas for flowers in the yard. A small, intimate space, just off the front walk, was designed to highlight a modest garden statue, which is viewed as you come up the front walk, rather than from the street. Additional plantings at the public sidewalk near the edge of the property also help screen the statue from the road.

3.20

Figure 3.20.
A little touch of enclosure can go a long way in creating a sense of both privacy and comfort. This picket fence very effectively embraces the front entrance of the home.

Figure 3.21.
The stone retaining wall, fence, and planting create an area to develop a front entrance garden while adding depth and interest to the narrow front yard.

TIP

While screen plantings obscure unwanted views and add privacy, they shouldn't inspire comments like, "Hey! Nice 10 ft. hedge." The variety of plants in the screen should be beautiful to look at while providing privacy for your property.

One thing to note about successful screen plantings: although they obscure unwanted views and add privacy, they shouldn't inspire comments like "Hey! Nice 10 ft. hedge." A successful plant screen considers both form and function. The variety of plants in the screen should be beautiful to look at while providing privacy for the property.

Finally, even though a lot of the design work at the Schulenburgs' focused on gardening and privacy, the Schulenburgs' children's interest in the landscape wasn't overlooked. The design also incorporates the front lawn as a space for games and activities.

Success story. The success of this landscape makeover was felt wholeheartedly when the Schulenburgs put their house up for sale in the thick of a buyer's market. The house, with its eye-catching architecture and complementary landscaping, sold quickly. The Schulenburgs are believers in the importance of beautiful, logical landscaping. They have invested in design projects at each of the four subsequent homes they have since owned.

4

FRONT GARDEN MAKEOVER
BEAUTY AND THE BASICS: THE KRUPKE HOUSE

3.22

3.23

Oftentimes when a builder is eager to close on a house and move on to the next project, a routine slate of building and landscaping elements are put in place: attached garage on the left side of the house; a curved, 3 ft. wide front walk just a few feet from the garage; and a little mustache of bowling ball–shaped plants smashed up against the foundation of the house. It's efficient and typical and often found in suburban developments.

The Krupke house had been the recipient of all of these builder shortcuts. As homeowners, we ought to demand a little more thoughtfulness for our money, as this style of landscape adds no depth or interest to the property. Here's how the Krupkes broke free from the typical design found throughout American suburbia.

Places for plants. The existing 3 ft. wide walk, which forced visitors to walk single file, was removed to make space for a more inviting 4 ft. wide walk, which included an expanded area for congregating. This kind of expanded area is an important design

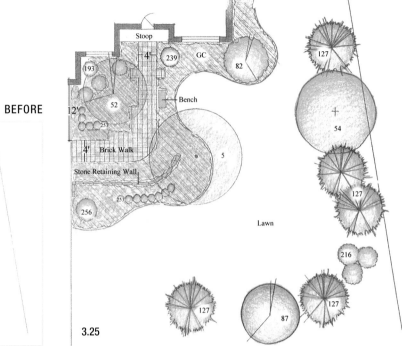

Residence

Stoop

4"

239

GC

82

193

Bench

12'

52

BEFORE

253

4' Brick Walk

5

Stone Retaining Wall

253

256

127

54

127

216

127

87

Lawn

3.25

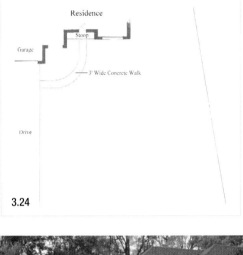

Residence

Stoop

Garage

3' Wide Concrete Walk

Drive

3.24

3.26

element because it adds interest and depth to the front walk, while providing a little space to greet and bid farewell to guests.

The new walk was located 11 ft. from the garage to create a space for a significant planting between the garage and the entrance walk. Planting areas are an important part of any landscape design. They allow space for plantings that are beautiful, compelling, and useful. They help soften hard surfaces, add depth and dimension, create a garden setting, and subtly break up large areas.

You don't have to be a master gardener to make a larger planting area beautiful. Gardening isn't a priority for the Krupkes, so they kept their plant list simple and minimized the space dedicated to high-maintenance flowers. The use of groundcover helps unify the garden, creating a nice flow throughout, and provides year-round foliage.

A planting was also added at the perimeter of the property to further screen the view of the neighbor's house and the cul-de-sac pavement.

Figure 3.26.
This screen planting around the perimeter of the property will ultimately provide screening of the neighbor's garage and drive.

Figures 3.27 and 3.28.
This low retaining wall is not only functional but also provides interest as viewed from the inside of the house (3.28).

One great wall. To correct a slight grade change from the street to the home, a low-profile, 18 in. tall retaining wall was built. This wall, which faces the house, accomplishes two things. It helps divert the flow of water away from the home. Also, the wall frames the entrance garden, adding beauty and interest to the space whether you're relaxing there in the outdoors or admiring the space from inside the house.

The payoff. Three years after landscaping this home, the Krupkes had to move. They attributed the quick sale of their home to the quality and beauty of the landscape.

CHAPTER 4

Retreat and

The Back Garden

When you look at your backyard, what do you see? A tapestry of beautiful gardens and patios? Perhaps a lush expanse of precisely mown lawn? A refuge for wildlife? Does it soothe the senses with a relaxing pool and spa? Or is it a sports haven, with athletic equipment of every kind?

Your backyard is the part of your property's landscape you'll use most often. Whether you have a garden, a sports center, or both, the landscape should reflect your particular lifestyle and interests. Also consider your backyard an extension of your home and the perfect opportunity to coordinate the exterior style with your interior design.

When you set out to design this private swatch of landscape, aim to please your family. If you have children, for instance, a precisely trimmed hedge and high-maintenance flower beds probably aren't for you. Instead, a few easy-to-care-for plants and lawn space for a fleet of battery-powered toys or fanciful childhood games is in order.

Whatever your whim, from swing sets to sweet peas, the backyard is the place for it.

For most families the backyard is the place for both retreat and recreation. Consider the following examples of spaces you can create in your backyard: room to entertain, a place to cook, play space for the family, and a relaxing escape.

Room 1: Party platform

When you're entertaining outdoors, a patio, a deck, or a gazebo is an ideal space for merrymaking.

Deck. A deck is essential if you have to make a house-to-yard transition from a higher point to a lower one. Consider the case of a home with a back door that is several feet—or even an entire level—above the ground. A deck can be essential in giving you and your guests a way to exit the main level of your house, then descend to a larger patio surface that serves as the main gathering space in your garden. This type of deck requires a railing for safety, and the deck should be kept to a minimal size to reduce its impact on the landscape.

When designing a deck, consider its appearance and the views from not only the deck itself but also from inside your house. For the best views indoors and out, keep the deck as low profile as possible, in an effort to minimize the use of railings. This will help your deck blend into your landscape. A deck surrounded by railings often takes on the look of a fishing pier, and those railings tend to block the sight lines to the rest of your beautiful garden, especially when you're taking in the view from inside your house.

Patio. A staple in nearly all garden designs, a patio is generally preferable to a deck because it allows for more flexibility and creativity in your landscape. Virtually nothing is out of the question for materials when it comes to patios: poured concrete, brick, and natural stone are all options, though brick is the most widely used.

A good size for most patios is 300 sq. ft. The space is sufficient for most gardens and gatherings because it provides ample room to entertain without leaving you feeling as though you've been stranded in the middle of an oversized parking lot. If, however, you tend to host very large gatherings, you may prefer a patio as much as two to three times this size.

Regardless of size, the location and design of the patio are paramount. Beware the kidney bean–shaped patio. The once-novel shape might have complemented the

Figure 4.1.
This brick patio, located outside of the kitchen doors, is of a size that meets the needs of the family and makes them feel like part of the garden.

landscape it was first designed for, but if there's no link to your own landscape, it's not the best design solution. In our experience the kidney bean–shaped design complements very few, if any, home styles.

If having backyard space both for entertaining and as a private retreat is important to you, consider creating multiple patios. The larger patio, off the main entertaining area of the house, could be complemented with a smaller, more intimate patio, which is to be used most often by your immediate household. Multiple surfaces should be constructed by paths or walks to allow people to move from one to the other when you entertain guests. A smaller surface can maintain its intimate, private appeal by if you create planting pockets to separate the two surfaces but still make the smaller surface accessible from the large surface by a walk.

Gazebo. Making for a cozy, private retreat in the backyard, a gazebo offers a comfortable way to enjoy the outdoors while providing a little shelter from the elements. Gazebos come in a wide array of styles and sizes; be sure to choose one that is in keeping with the scale, style, and theme of your garden. Finding the right spot for the gazebo is important, too. Like every element in your yard, it needs to fit in and coordinate with the other structures and plantings. A common mistake is to place the gazebo right in the middle of the yard, but that cleaves the landscape in two. Placing the gazebo on the perimeter opens up the space in your garden to make room for a complete composition of plantings, lawn, walkways, and other gathering spots.

Room 2: Outdoor kitchen

Entertaining outdoors often leads to eating outdoors. Soon enough, you realize the logistics for your outdoor parties would be much simpler if only you could cook out there, too.

Enter the outdoor kitchen. Your cooking area can be as simple as a fire pit or as elaborate as your in-home setup, complete with refrigerator and kitchen sink.

Creating an outdoor kitchen and planning the surrounding space will require extra care and additional design expertise. When tackling a large, detailed project such as this, consulting a landscape architect or landscape designer would be beneficial. As with any professional, do your research and get a referral. Not only can these pros give you great ideas and advice, but they can also give you great recommendations for other professionals (masons, carpenters, plumbers, etc.) who can help you with your project.

If an old-fashioned wiener roast is your idea of cooking in the great outdoors, then a fire pit is the way to go. A fire pit can be a portable or permanent fixture in the landscape. With either type of fire pit, you'll benefit from the dual purpose of cooking tasty meals and staying cozy on chilly nights.

Place a portable fire pit in any safe location when firing it up, and then put it away when not in use, so you have more space to move about. Construct a permanent fire pit of stone and install it either above or below ground. Its design should complement the patio and the style and materials of the surrounding landscape to ensure that it does not become a distraction when not in use.

A third alternative for outdoor cooking: Make space for a grill just off the main entertaining surface. In most cases, simply accommodating a grill in your patio or deck design will meet your cooking needs while giving you a more versatile entertaining area.

Room 3: Play space

From a playhouse for the little ones to an athletic venue for the older kids (including you), the backyard is the place to play. Similar to creating an outdoor kitchen, you can create a space that is as simple or as elaborate as your preferences demand.

A straightforward, open area of lawn is an ideal space for active play, for a swing set or play set, or for croquet or bocce ball. A few plantings, strategically placed, link your lawn to the overall landscape. Design your planting areas around the perimeter of the yard, allowing the interior lawn space to be used for active play.

More elaborate play spaces could include a full basketball or tennis court. Areas such as these should be located away from the main garden area. Otherwise, they can quickly overpower a landscape and make it appear more city park than private backyard.

Room 4: Great escape

A pool or spa will offer a resort-like escape in your own backyard. These large structures deliver big on relaxation, and they command a similar amount of attention in your landscape. That's why they must be a major consideration in your landscape planning to ensure a beautiful design. It is nearly impossible to force a pool or spa into an inappropriate space or to retrofit an existing landscape to accommodate one. If your plans call for a pool or spa to be added to your landscape sometime in the future, make space for it now.

The patio and pool are best designed as a unit, and accounting for this before any work is done is essential. A spa, while smaller, is still a tough fit without careful planning. Aboveground units can be especially tricky, but good location and the right plantings can help integrate one into your landscape design.

A word of caution: Give careful consideration to whether a pool or spa is something you really want. Many a homeowner has gone to the expense and trouble of installing one, only to discover that the novelty soon wears off and the maintenance required is anything but relaxing.

EXTERIOR DESIGN

Your backyard is an extension of your home. Whether it includes a gazebo for entertaining or a pool for relaxing, your outdoor space should coordinate with both the interior design and the architecture of your home. The result will be a unified, beautiful feel throughout your property.

4.2

Figure 4.2.
This patio surface connects two doors and leads to paths around the home. The complimentary shape of the surface is in scale with the house.

Furnishings. Furnish an outdoor room with the care and attention you would use in decorating inside your home. Choose a visual theme and stick to it. Find quality furniture that suits your taste and fits your home's style. A potpourri of patio furniture is distracting, and it detracts from the look and feel you are trying to achieve. Think of it like this: just because the furniture is outdoors doesn't mean it ought to look like it came from your college dorm room.

There are as many options for outdoor furniture as there are shades of beige for your living room couch. Materials range from wood-and-iron combos to woven products. Many are available with cushions and fabrics that rival those of your favorite couch (beige or otherwise). In a private garden, a simple bistro set with two chairs and a small table is often just the right touch. In a larger setting, a table-and-chair set much like that in your dining room lets larger groups dine in comfort outdoors. For sunny climes umbrellas are available to match your furniture design and fabric.

Personal style. The backyard is an ideal place to show off your personal style. Garden art or statuary, outdoor furnishings, fountains, or ponds personalize your garden and reflect your unique tastes.

Art and statuary pieces, coming in every shape and size, may add a touch of mystery, class, or whimsy to the garden. A word of caution, though: the key to attractive ornamentation is restraint, as too much of a good thing will ruin your carefully designed landscape. A garden can easily become cluttered with art and statuary. A single piece is often more effective and pleasing to the eye than rows of statues and urns. Carefully chosen and thoughtfully placed, such an ornament can become a focal point in the garden, highlight an area of interest, or direct attention away from something less desirable, such as an electrical box.

Figure 4.3.
The careful placement of this little lamb gives the appearance that it is a natural part of the garden.

4.3

A place for plants. Spacing between elements affects the feel and flow of your outdoor room. With a patio or deck, for instance, be sure to leave space between that surface and the foundation of your home. This is a simple design technique that shows off both your outdoor gathering space and your home to its greatest advantage. The separation gives you room for plantings that make the transition between the low, horizontal deck and the vertical wall. The result is greater depth and more visual interest from all vantage points, whether you're standing in the midst of your garden or enjoying the view from inside your house.

Easy access. Access is everything. Being able to move through the yard and experience all it has to offer should be a delight. Nobody wants to go navigate a rocky, worn-out path or squishy ground. Include walkways and garden paths to make it easy for your family and guests to get to the main gathering spaces. Walkways leading from

On the level
Most of us are not fortunate enough to have level lots for our homes and gardens. In fact, some properties are so sloping that a garden may seem like an impossibility. Thus, the retaining wall. This simple garden edifice can turn a ski slope into a series of beautiful terraced areas with patios and lawn.

4.4

Figure 4.4.
This bridge leads to another part of the garden. The bridge crosses a swale that would otherwise have lawn.

the front of the home to the back provide access to the garden other than through your house—an ideal solution for cutting down on the dirt that kids will track into the house or for giving visitors a beeline to your garden party. Within the garden, walkways and paths should unite separate areas where there will be a lot of foot traffic that lawn and groundcover cannot withstand.

Paths and walkways can do so much more for your landscape than simply move folks from point A to point B. Your garden paths should be as beautiful as they are useful. An alluring serpentine flagstone path becomes an attractive landscape feature in its own right, as well as serving the purpose of linking separate areas of the garden.

A trip down your garden lane should be an experience, perhaps even revealing some garden delights—a fountain, statuary, a small, unique planting.

Landscape lighting. There's no reason to abandon your garden when the sun goes down. Use landscape lighting to enhance the nighttime beauty of the garden and to extend your time enjoying the backyard. To revisit a common theme in landscaping, though: moderation is a wonderful thing. Don't be tempted to cast light everywhere in a misguided effort to turn night into day. Lighting your yard like a football stadium on game day is not only unattractive but also cruel to your neighbors and wildlife.

Subtle lighting can create dramatic effects. Patio, deck, and pathways should be lit for safety and ease of use. A few lights for each will provide ample coverage. Avoid lighting every square inch, however, as that creates an overdone runway effect.

Light plants with the same care. Pick a few key plants and then experiment with different lighting techniques to discover what works best for your garden. Plants can be lit from above, below, in front, or behind. Pay attention not only to the light created by different techniques but also to the shadows.

Privacy, please. To truly relax in your backyard, you'll want to protect your space and create some privacy. That doesn't mean you have to put up the Berlin Wall. Creating a sense of enclosure, rather than entrapment, is the goal. Undesirable objects, such as the neighbor's garbage cans, need to be screened from a patio that you use frequently to entertain. A distant view of a majestic oak tree, on the other hand, is one worth maintaining.

Screening can be achieved with proper plantings. A combination of taller plants in the back and smaller plants in the front of a planting brings privacy without making a wall. Using a variety of evergreens and deciduous plants will help bring seasonal interest to the garden, as well.

Trellises and pergolas can also be erected to screen unwanted views, particularly when used in combination with climbing plants. Either can be made of metal or wood and painted or stained to complement your exterior design. A trellis works well as a screen for an air conditioner, trash cans, and a neighbor's too-close-for-comfort window. A trellis can also add visual interest to a large expanse of wall. A pergola can become the focal point for the entire garden, while simultaneously screening unwanted views and providing shade for a sitting area.

Like a pergola, fencing can serve as a design element as well as a reliable screen. A short fence can help define different areas of the garden. A tall privacy fence may be the solution for screening when space is at a premium. You may love your neighbors dearly, but after all, waving to them every five minutes while trying to enjoy a quiet evening on the patio can be frustrating.

HOW DOES YOUR GARDEN GROW?

Plants unite your entire landscape. Forming a plan and knowing your flora style can help you create a composition of plants, while avoiding a collection of specimen plants that together do nothing for your landscape. A plan will also help you avoid the impulse buy every time you visit the garden center.

A well-rounded composition of plants should include taller plants and ornamental trees toward the back of a planting, with shrubs and groundcovers toward the front. Plant beds should have a meandering shape to create a natural feeling. This creates dimension and avoids the wall effect that many homeowners have planted in their backyards. Incorporating both evergreens and deciduous plants adds seasonal interest to the composition.

If you can plant only a few plants first, begin with the larger trees, rather than plant a few shrubs that have little effect on the landscape as a whole. Trees have the greatest impact on the landscape and take the longest to grow. Getting them in first will give you a jump start on a beautiful garden. In the future, as time, interest, and money allow, you can add the smaller garden elements to complete the composition.

Right plant, right place. One piece of advice will see you through nearly every plant decision you make: put the right plant in the right place. In contrast, as soon as a plant is placed in a poor location, it is doomed. In the wrong soil or light conditions, it will perform poorly or die. In a too-small space, a plant will become a maintenance nightmare, as you constantly have to prune it to keep it small. Ultimately, the over-pruned plant will fail.

So, how do you pick the right plant and the right place? First consider the space you have available and the sun exposure that spot receives. Size and sun are the first and most important characteristics to consider when evaluating a plant and its place. All too often a large shrub can be found positioned 2 ft. from the foundation of a house, underneath a window. While the shrub might look nice when first planted, problems will most certainly occur during the first couple of years. Soon branches will be squashed against the house, blocking the view from the window. Properly planting the same shrub 8 ft. from the house might make it appear small and insignificant at first, but in time your patience will be rewarded with a beautiful, healthy plant that enhances your landscape for years.

Knowing what kind of space and sun exposure you have to work with, choose a plant that will thrive in those conditions. A quality plant should provide seasonal interest throughout the year, even as the seasons change. Characteristics that provide this year-round interest include flowers, fruit, foliage, fall foliage, texture, and branching structure. Do you want plants that attract birds and wildlife? Is a formal garden or natural woodland area more appropriate? How much maintenance can you do?

Finally, when selecting a beautiful, high-quality plant, avoid those that are brightly colored, have variegated leaves, weeping branches, contorted branches, or any combination of these. Plants like this are distracting. They shout out for attention and detract from the other plants in the landscape. Understandably, you may be intrigued by such sensational plants, but they are usually one-dimensional. What you see is what you get, and as the seasons change, the novelty the plant once had wears off. A small allowance: If you simply must have one of these specialty plants, place it in your backyard as you would a garden ornament, but give it even less prominence. Why? Such plants are not known for their longevity, and one can truly become an eyesore as it dies off.

Trees. Trees with multiple stems are much more effective than the single-stemmed tree in the landscape. While your gaze drifts right past a single-stemmed tree or sees it as a stick in the mud, a tree with several stems holds a compelling shape and your attention, no matter what the season. Multiple-stemmed trees are also useful for screening unsightly views and for increasing privacy.

Single-stem trees do have their place in the landscape. Parkway trees, for instance, need to be single stemmed for vehicle and pedestrian clearance. Many shade trees near patio areas should also be single stemmed, so as to avoid obstructing a desirable view of your landscape.

Flowers. If you love splashes of color in the garden, flowerbeds are the way to go. Annuals, perennial flowers, and bulbs add year-round color. If you make flowers a part

Figure 4.5.
This multiple-stemmed tree provides more privacy and a more interesting structure than the typical single-stemmed tree. When lighting is used at night, it will create a wonderful shadow on walls.

4.5

of your garden, commit to treating them well. Flowers increase the amount of maintenance and watering that your landscape will require. Most flowers will require watering, particularly when planted in containers. Vegetable and herb gardens, which also add color and fragrance to a yard, offer similar beauty and require similar levels of care.

FROM ANY VANTAGE POINT

The well-planned back garden is appealing from any vantage point. Whether you're admiring the landscape from your kitchen window or standing in the midst of it, the back garden should beckon you outdoors. Once there, you should feel welcomed by all the style and appeal you'd expect of the interior living and entertaining spaces in your home.

TIP

Peaceful pond

A fountain or pond can express your personal style, while adding soothing sound or tranquil water to the garden. It's essential that your pond blend well with its natural surroundings. Organic shapes and varying sizes of boulders and smaller rocks help create a natural feel. Each rock should be placed individually with great attention to detail, in order to achieve the best effect. A few well-placed plants, and the pond will look like it belongs.

That kind of careful planning will help you avoid creating a pond that looks as though somebody just dug a hole, dumped some rock, and then filled the whole thing with water. Also, be sure you're passionate about having a pond. As with swimming pools, there is a significant amount of maintenance required, and if you neglect it, your pond will quickly become an eyesore in your otherwise beautiful landscape.

1

BEFORE

GARDEN PARTY: THE ANGELL HOUSE

4.6

4.7

The Angells are avid gardeners who enjoy entertaining. Their home, in the northern suburbs of Chicago, was built in the 1940s. Due to the house's small size, the owners decided to expand it and improve their landscaping. The backyard, they said, needed a stronger sense of privacy, since the neighboring property was too close to their beautiful space for entertaining guests. The landscaping also needed to address a drainage problem. But first things first: Before any landscaping took place, the existing shed on the west side of the house was removed, and a sunroom and a porch were added.

Planting a small space. Because the Angells have no children and planned to entertain only small groups of people, their limited backyard space is ideal. Approximately 30 by 40 ft., the yard gets its courtyard feeling from being enclosed by the walls of the house and the neighbors' fencing. A brick patio, in the middle of the yard, is tucked into a lush garden setting. The array of plants helps break up the hard surfaces of the surrounding walls and fencing, and delights the Angells, who come from a family of garden enthusiasts. There is not a single blade of grass in this garden, and more than 25% of the yard is planted with flowers.

The privacy factor. Because of the closeness of the neighboring homes and an alley, adding privacy to this garden was a priority. The lush garden surrounding the patio provides screening to distinctly separate the Angells' property from the neighbors'.

BEFORE

A great wall. Boulder walls, one free-standing (4.12) and one retaining (4.11), were built in the yard. From a functional perspective, the walls divert water flow away from the home and address the grade issue. In terms of form, the walls add visual interest and dimension to the courtyard.

Figures 4.8 through 4.10. This once sterile backyard (4.10) was transformed into an intimate garden with privacy and year-round interest created with seasonal color and a mix of woody and evergreen plants.

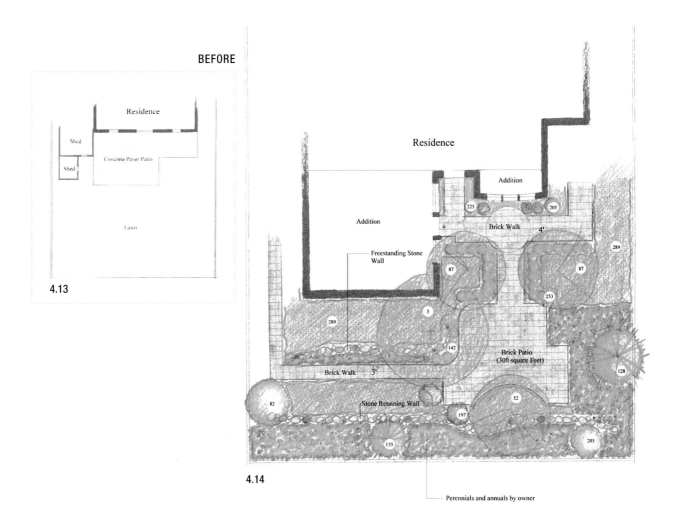

BEFORE

4.13

4.14

Perennials and annuals by owner

The transformation. The appearance of the Angells' home was completely transformed. With the shed and all the existing landscape removed, space was made for new hardscapes and plantings (4.15 and 4.16). One of the owners, an interior designer, applied her keen eye for design to the landscape and made it an ever-changing piece of art. Ultimately, the detailed design of this small outdoor living area created an intimate, charming, and usable courtyard in a restricted space.

2

BACK GARDEN MAKEOVER
BACKYARD BEAUTY: THE MIGLEY HOUSE

The Migleys' historical home was set on a semi-wooded lot in a cozy old-time town. The one blemish on this picturesque arrangement was the Migley backyard. They had a tiny deck with space enough for only the two of them, and it looked out over a sea of, well, not much. The result was an awkward "fishing pier" appearance. Large railings surrounding the deck created a claustrophobic setting. The back of the Migley house was exposed to the neighboring property, and their own main view was of their garage. The long, sterile expanse of walls wasn't much of a backdrop for mornings spent relaxing outdoors or for evenings spent entertaining.

The view. With plans for adding a new patio, the Migleys decided the little deck could stay. We would have liked to have either removed or redesigned the deck, but due to costs and the access it provided to the backyard, the deck stayed. Due to the height of the deck and our concern for safety, we also left the railing intact. However, while the deck was once the gathering place, now it merely provides access to the

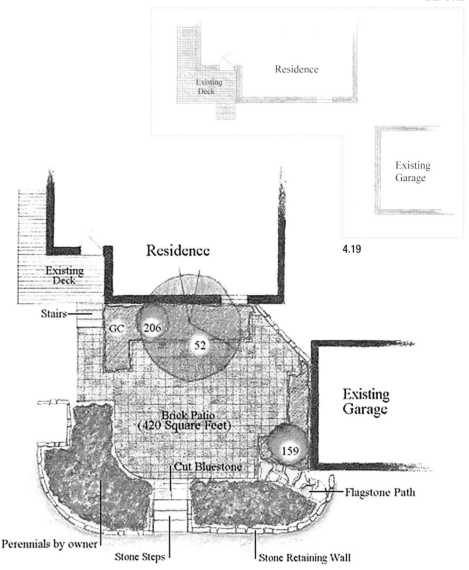

4.19

4.20

When designing retaining walls that surround a usable surface, such as a patio, be sure to allow space between the wall and the surface for a garden planting.

much larger—and nicer—main entertaining space below. Moving directly off the deck, an entirely new garden was designed between the house and the garage. Plantings surrounding the patio gave the area a comfortable, cozy feeling. They helped visibly interrupt the large blank walls of the home and garage while maintaining views of the semi-wooded property from indoors.

All walled up. A stone retaining wall was built to level out an area of the yard and provide an enclosed space for the backyard garden. Inside the retaining wall, a new brick patio was designed to give the Migleys space to relax and to entertain. A garden of plants and flowers was installed between the patio and the retaining wall.

4.21

Figures 4.21 through 4.23. As enjoyable as flowers are, they don't bloom all year long. When the annuals are gone and perennials are dormant, it is important to have woody plants to add structure and interest to the garden. Imagine the different views from this patio in the late fall or early spring with no structural elements—very drab.

Plants with purpose. The Migleys chose an assortment of flowers for their garden, and they opted to add some woody plants. When the flowers are dormant, the woody plants will provide visual interest. The planting accomplishes two other things. It softens the hard surfaces and creates a gardenlike setting. Second, the pocket of planting acts as a safety barrier between the often-used patio and the drop-off beyond the retaining wall.

4.22

Design for success. As the Migleys' landscape plans were developed, the couple took into account their circumstances. They had no children, so open lawn space wasn't a requirement. They did have a steeply sloped yard and some privacy issues to address. That led them to their design goals: creating a sizable back garden area where they could entertain guests, enjoy gardening outdoors, and improve their views.

4.23

Pleased with the success of this initial design, the Migleys continued to develop their landscape through the years. And when they moved to a new home, attending to the landscape design was one of the first things they did, so they could best enjoy their property.

ROOM TO GROW: THE KEMP HOUSE

4.24

When the Kemp family put an addition onto their home, they faced a common situation that most homeowners overlook: building onto your home changes your landscape and how you use it. The Kemps enjoyed cooking outdoors and spending family time there. They also liked to entertain in their backyard. They wanted a backyard that would suit both kinds of activities in this now-smaller area.

Getting started. The solution to the Kemps' landscape problem was to design a garden with two distinct areas: a public space for entertaining the neighbors and a more private area for personal use. First, though, a substantial grade had to be addressed. A stone retaining wall corrected the grade and created a large, usable area. Then the two separate surfaces were designed for it.

Two new rooms. The two new spaces were planned as extensions of rooms inside the home. The first surface, used for grilling, is a smaller, private space that is accessed from the owners' kitchen. This 770 sq. ft. area is tucked into a corner created by the house. The result is a cozy, intimate space ideal for family dining and relaxing.

4.25

4.26

4.27

The larger room, approximately 900 sq. feet, is accessed directly off the living area. This area was designed for entertaining larger groups.

Both outdoor rooms are surfaced with brick pavers. Plants play a critical role in creating a sense of separation between the two outdoor rooms. To access the rest of the yard easily, six flagstone steps were built into the retaining wall.

A warm welcome. The spaces between the stone walls and patios are planting pockets. The woody plants and flowers cultivated there soften the surrounding hard surfaces and make the rooms feel cozy and inviting.

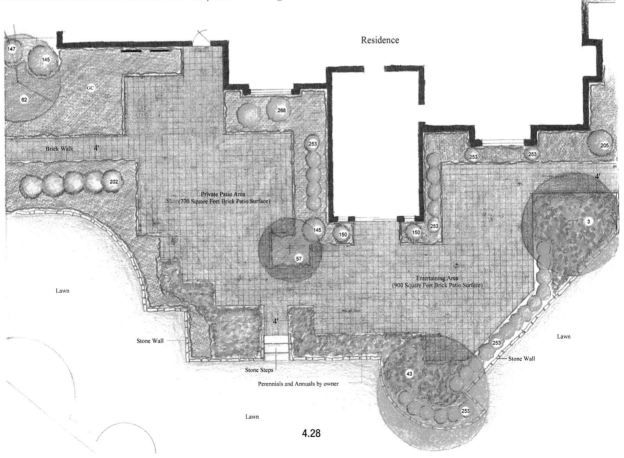

4.28

A WOODED RETREAT: THE GOLITZ HOUSE

4.29

4.30

The Golitz home sits on five wooded acres. Through the years the homeowners had transformed their landscape into a series of small gardens, which ultimately looked dated. Empty nesters who love to entertain, the Golitzes wanted to redesign their main patio and reinvent the backyard area.

Trouble on deck. The family's wooden deck was a trouble spot in their backyard. It crowded the entrance to their home, blocked the view from indoors, and required a lot of maintenance. Surrounded by steps, the deck was meant to have an open, spacious feeling. The usable space actually shrank in size, however, as people stayed a good distance away from the edge of the deck: being too close to that first step made folks feel like they might tumble off the deck. And the patio below was made of street pavers that had become uneven over time, so that surface wasn't very inviting, either. Ultimately, the deck and surrounding patio failed to provide a truly functional space and comfortable setting because they were at different levels.

Plants and planters without purpose. Too much maintenance in a garden can quickly turn a thing of beauty into a black hole for time spent on chores and repairs.

Such was the case with the existing plants and planters. The plants were old, overgrown, and in some areas overpruned. The raised wood planters were in disrepair, too, and that further detracted from the plants and the overall appeal of the landscape. The Golitzes also had a collection of interesting art pieces in their garden, but the shoddiness of the surroundings eclipsed their beauty.

The new design. The redesign began with an excavation: the wooden deck, planters, and patio were removed. In place of the deck, a cut flagstone patio was installed. The natural material of the flagstone patio is more pleasing to the eye, and it fits in better with the landscape. The street pavers from the old patio were relocated to surround the new flagstone area, extending the surface to an 800 sq. ft. space, which is ideal for entertaining. By combining the two spaces into one and eliminating the drop-off that had existed between the deck and the patio, the space is now much more comfortable and functional.

4.31

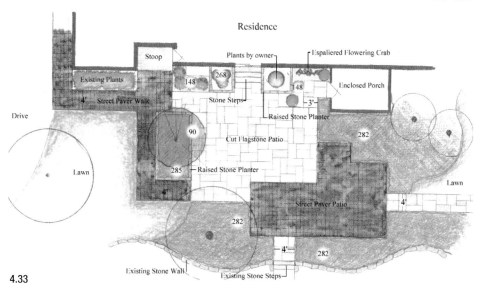

4.32

BEFORE

Figure 4.31.
The original seating areas were on different levels and not at all functional. With the new design, the surfaces were combined at one level, providing a great deal of flexibility for entertaining. Using two different materials helps to visually break up the large area.

4.33

Figures 4.34 and 4.35.
The raised stone planters are doubly functional, retaining the steps and providing an attractive setting for the plants, both in the planters (4.35) and next to them at ground level (4.34).

4.34

4.35

Raised planters around the doorway and patio were constructed from flagstone, which is superior to wood in both beauty and durability. The planters around the door create small, charming planting areas while also serving as a retaining wall that supports the stone steps leading from the door.

Planting areas situated between the patio and the house help soften the hard surfaces and add beauty to the garden. To bring the beauty of the back garden into the house, as well, planting areas were located under and around windows and French doors. When the Golitzes look out from inside, the beauty of the garden—rather than just the hard surfaces—is easily seen.

4.36

4.37

Finally, the pieces of the garden art collection have been thoughtfully arranged throughout the garden. They are strategically placed—some obvious, some almost hidden as little surprises—to add beauty and to delight visitors to the Golitz garden. One key piece of the collection, a beautiful fountain, was placed on the small hill behind the patio so it could easily be seen and enjoyed from the patio.

4.38

Figures 4.36 through 4.38. The fountain is viewed on an axis from the patio, while the stone piece (4.38), situated amongst shrubs, is viewed in a more natural setting.

A flagstone path leads from the patio to the fountain. Beyond the yard the property resumes its natural wooded characteristic. The landscaping in the yard now provides a smooth transition from the carefully cultivated backyard to the natural woodland.

CHAPTER 5

Harmony

The Master Plan

Before you make any improvements to your landscape, you must create a master plan for developing your current landscape into your dream landscape. Why? The master plan covers your entire landscape, from front to back and everything in between. Rather than design your landscape in chunks over time and hope it all fits together in the end, address the landscape as a whole with a master plan. It will unify the front, back, and side yards, so that functionality and a sense of style will prevail. It will become your guide to making decisions about your home's landscape, now and in the future.

IMAGINE YOUR DREAM LANDSCAPE

What do you envision as your ultimate landscape? Ask yourself, What do I want in my landscape? What major elements, such as walks, surfaces, and retaining walls, do I need? How would these features work with my home's layout? Do I want some shade or flower color? How much lawn do I want? How much maintenance can I handle? How can I incorporate my personal style? Do I want a formal garden with tightly trimmed hedges and perfectly manicured lawn, or do I prefer a natural garden that attracts birds, butterflies, and other wildlife?

Along with imagining the look and feel of your garden, consider what areas need improvement. Are there problem spots in your yard, like low-lying areas that flood when it rains or a steep slope in part of the yard that makes the space unusable? Issues like drainage and grading need to be corrected before any design work is done. Another issue to consider is screening: Will you need planting to screen unpleasant views or to increase privacy? Considering issues like these can help you create a clear picture of what the right landscape looks like for you.

So, take some time to contemplate your dream landscape. Make a list of your landscape needs and dreams. Don't forget the practical side of planning. Consider the questions and elements in the following lists.

How do you plan to spend your time in your yard?

Entertaining

How much space will you need?

Do you like to have large parties with a lot of people, or do you usually have casual gatherings of a few people?

Do you need an area for grilling?

A good way to determine how large an outdoor surface you need for entertaining is to find a room in your house that you use for entertaining and that feels comfortable—for example, your living or dining room. These rooms usually hold a table and chairs for entertaining guests—elements usually needed outside, too!—so they are good size references for an outdoor surface. Measure the rooms and translate those figures to your landscape. Generally, 200 sq. ft. is a bit small outdoors, and 400 sq. ft. can be rather large. (We have, however, developed patios in excess of 800 sq. ft.)

Playing sports and using open space

What sports do you play?

How much lawn space will you need?

Do you need a field or a court?

Relaxing

Do you want to use your garden as a getaway?

Do you need privacy screening?

TIP

If you don't have a green thumb and you're worried about how much garden maintenance and other yard work you can handle, start small. You can always add more plants later.

Are there any unsightly views that you want to screen?

Do you want any water elements or statuary in your garden?

Enjoying the weather

Are there areas that need shade?

Adding color

Where do you want to add some color?

Are you an avid gardener?

How much maintenance are you willing to do?

Do you prefer one bold splash of color, or a mixture?

Getting out at night

Do you need lighting?

What kind of lighting, and how much?

Does it get cool?

Do you want a fire pit?

What structural elements will be needed in your yard?

Patio	Garden shed	Croquet court
Walks	Arbor	Putting green
Grill or other cooking area	Fencing	Tree house
Fire pit	Sculpture	Swing set
Pool	Basketball court	Dog run
Spa	Tennis court	Clothesline
Water features	Baseball diamond	

CREATE A MASTER PLAN

Once you know what you want and need in your landscape, you can start the process toward reality by putting it all down on paper. Start by loosely sketching out your ideas, maybe in a bubble diagram. There is no need for a lot of detail at this point. Just get your ideas on paper, so you can visualize the future connections between various areas in your landscape (fig. 5.1).

Grab a sketch pad and a pencil. Before designing anything, indicate the location of all permanent elements and structures, such as the house, property lines, garden shed, fences, driveway, public sidewalk, and large shade trees. Begin the future design by sketching in the larger elements of the hardscape: place the walks, patio surfaces, and any retaining walls that are needed. Entrances, recreational areas, screen planting, and any other features for your particular garden should all be included. As your sketch evolves, you can add refine it with details like the specific size and shape of the patio and the locations of smaller planting areas.

When developing your master plan, focus first on the big picture. Indicate where you'd like the major components— patios, walks, planting areas, lawn—to go. Don't worry about the specific details yet. If you plan to develop your landscape in phases over time, you don't need to know the variety and size of every last plant or accessory you hope to include.

Figure 5.1.
A simple sketch or
bubble diagram is a
good way to visualize
your dream landscape.

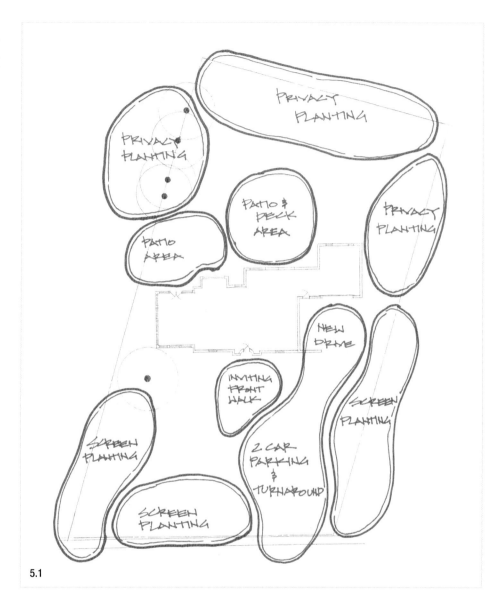

5.1

With sketch in hand, head outdoors. Take along string, stakes, and spray paint to help transfer the sketch from paper to your property. Lay out the major design elements in the yard as you drew them on paper. What looks good on paper doesn't always hold up in the real world. Seeing each feature's preliminary layout right in the landscape will help you determine a better location, perhaps, and fine-tune its size. Now is the time to make changes to your plan. Stakes and string are much easier to relocate than flagstone and trees!

Give yourself some time in your stakes-and-string garden to be sure that the basic layout of the master plan works well with the space you have and complements the way you use your garden. Once everything is located and adjusted and sized to your satisfaction, record it all on paper in a more detailed drawing.

BUDGET FOR IMPROVEMENTS

There's no hard-and-fast rule to the common question, How much should I spend on landscaping my property? The general guideline, however, is 5–10% of the value of your home. Of course, a professional landscape designer might suggest that there is no amount too great for creating a beautiful yard. Keep the following points in mind as you prioritize your landscape needs and set your budget.

Intangible rewards. Investing in your garden will pay you back with a wealth of intangibles: a space that suits your family's needs, beauty in your own backyard, a comfortable place to enjoy the outdoors.

Curb appeal. Investing in your landscape will pay you back with curb appeal that may help you sell your home and even increase its value.

Further development. For many of the homeowners featured in the garden makeovers, they report that their gardens mean more to them than they anticipated, and that they have ended up developing more garden space, over time, than they ever imagined.

Phased development. You don't have to do everything at once. Implementing a garden in phases over a few years is very common. Developing a master plan will help you prioritize your projects and set your budget.

PLAN FOR THE FUTURE

If you live in a home for more than three years, you'll see both your life and your landscape change. In fact, your yard may serve a variety of functions over time. A family with toddlers, for instance, will need a safe outdoor play area. As the kids grow up, that small play area may need to be expanded into to a larger expanse of lawn for athletics. Your master plan should be flexible enough to accommodate your changing needs. For instance, by planting large trees and herbaceous plants on the perimeter of your property, you avoid breaking up the main part of a yard, preserving the chance to further develop the space later.

A landscape architect can help you create a final master plan with just the right mix of flexibility in your planting and structures. A designer can also guide you in setting a timeline for phasing in your landscaping plans, according to your budget limitations. First, though, the designer must know what elements you want in a yard and how you want to use and enjoy it. So, whether you decide to do it yourself or to work with a pro, the planning begins with you!

TIP

When creating your master plan, start by mapping out the locations and sizes of the hardscape: patio, walls, and walkways.

TIP

Your landscape should be a reflection of how you use it and what you want from it.

1

CLASSIC BEAUTY: THE SCHULENBURG HOUSE

5.2

5.3

The importance of good landscaping was not lost on the Schulenburgs, who had redesigned the front garden of a previous home. So, when they designed and built a new home, they knew a good landscape plan would help make the most of their investment. The Schulenburgs had the existing home razed, and in its place they constructed a Greek Revival home. Their research and meticulous attention to detail, including the design of working shutters, made the home look architecturally beautiful.

The challenge? The Schulenburgs were building a larger home than the one they had razed, making the lot seem relatively small. They needed to situate the house in a way that addressed the neighbors' concerns that it would look out of place, encroach on their properties, and even overwhelm them.

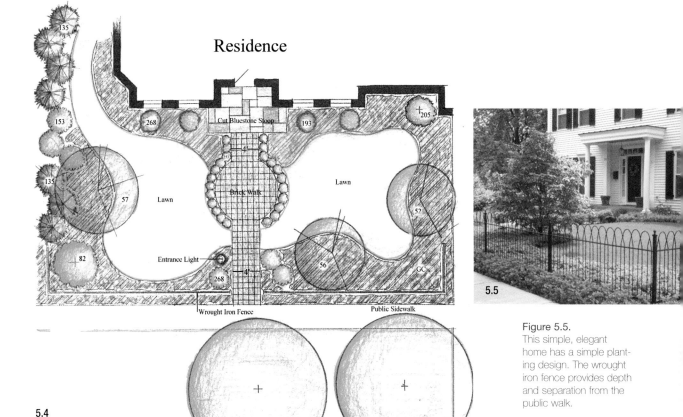

Residence

135

153

268   Cut Bluestone Stoop   193   205

4'

135   Lawn   Brick Walk   Lawn

57   52

82   Entrance Light   56   GC

268   4'

Wrought Iron Fence   Public Sidewalk

5.4

5.5

The front garden

The landscaping for the Schulenburg's new Greek Revival house began with the front entrance garden. Only 25 ft. separated the house from the public sidewalk. Despite the small space, the landscape plan created a sense of depth and made the entrance inviting. The front walk incorporated a circular surface where visitors could congregate as they arrived and departed. That circular space was kept in scale with the home, to maintain the sense of proportion and depth.

To set the stage and frame the entrance area, the circular surface was ringed with a simple evergreen boxwood hedge. To soften the lines of the house, plants were placed directly below the windows. They were carefully selected for their short stature, so they'd never obscure the view from inside.

The overall planting scheme for the front yard is very simple, and that was a key strategy in designing a beautiful landscape for this small space. Including too many varieties of plants would have cluttered the space rather than creating an elegant landscape that the eye can smoothly take in. The simple planting scheme made the most of the existing large shade trees in the parkway. A few small trees were added to help scale down the house and provide screening from the public sidewalk and road. Groundcover unifies the entire area and provides year-round color.

To further enclose the area, we designed a wrought iron fence for the yard. The fence is open and airy, which avoids making the small space feel smaller. The simple planting scheme is easy to appreciate from outside the fence, and the lush, beautiful landscape complements the classic style of the home. Still, the fence creates a sense of enclosure and separation from the street.

"Classic" is the key word here: This landscape would win approving glances as easily in 1887 or 1987 as today. Classics stand the test of time.

The back garden

This large-scale home on a small-scale lot leaves little room for a backyard. Nevertheless, the Schulenburgs wanted a garden area where they could sit and relax. Sticking to a few logical landscape principles made it possible to create a small patio that fit well, proportionally, with the house. With just a 300 sq. ft. patio, the design accommodated a few pieces of furniture and a few people. A neighboring property was just 12 ft. away from the edge of the patio, and the view was that of a tennis court fence. This made screening very important. Planting some large, narrow, shade-tolerant evergreens and a few small deciduous trees along the property line effectively provided screening, softened the look of the hard patio surface, and in general created a comfortable garden setting.

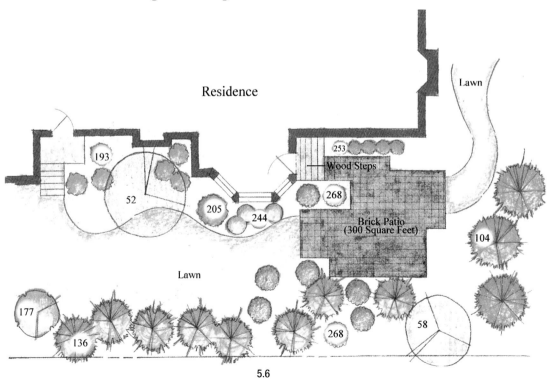

5.6

Figures 5.7 through 5.9. This surface is ideal for entertaining. The flower area is large enough to make a colorful impact, and privacy is attained through a carefully considered composition of plants.

5.7

5.8

5.9

TIP

When you have a small space, don't force a large variety of plant material into it. That would make the area look cluttered and distracting. Instead, keep the planting scheme simple.

Total harmony

Three years after the Schulenburgs' home was landscaped, it was chosen for the city's walk of historic homes. Although the house was new, its architectural style and detail made the house fit in perfectly with the surrounding historic neighborhood. The classic style of the home and its landscape won over the wary neighbors, who now consider it a neighborhood gem.

2

BEFORE

DESIGNED FOR COMFORT: THE DELCAMPO HOUSE

5.11

Over the course of twenty-five years, the DelCampo family has invested in landscape design for each of the four homes they've lived in. In 2000 they moved into the third of those four homes. This one was a fixer-upper, inside and out.

The front garden

Bringing beauty and cozy comfort to the front yard required major makeovers for the driveway, the front walk, and the plantings.

The driveway. The driveway had three major problems: It made a beeline right for the garage, rather than help give guests a warm welcome to the house. The driveway forced the DelCampo family and their visitors to back directly onto a busy road when leaving the house. And it was made of flagstone, which is a very nice material but almost never ideal for a driveway in the midwestern climate the DelCampos lived in.

Figure 5.13.
The driveway was realigned so that you could not see the garage door from the street. The beautiful European beech also helps soften the view of the garage.

BEFORE

The existing drive was removed so both driveway and front walk, which was also made of flagstone, could be redesigned. The new drive is located so that the view of the garage door is obscured, diminishing that hurry-up-and-park feeling. The drive now also includes two parking spaces. Those provide room for visitors to park and allow room for cars to turn around in the driveway, rather than having to back out onto the busy road.

The walk. A new bluestone front walk, starting adjacent to the visitor parking spaces, leads to the front door. Expanded areas of the front walk provide areas for visitors to gather, eliminating the need to stand in the driveway. A small patio area was also developed just off the front walk.

The entrance. Two freestanding walls, crafted from the old driveway's dug-up flagstone, define the front entrance. The walls create a courtyard setting there, providing separation between the driveway and the entrance. These walls are a great design element, adding interest and depth to the garden. The addition of custom-made wrought iron gates leading to the front entrance further define the space and emphasize separation between the parking spaces and front entrance surface. A custom-made wrought iron fence was also placed just inside the public sidewalk, framing the driveway entrance, to create a sense of enclosure.

A simple boxwood hedge—ideal because it can easily be pruned and kept small—frames the front entrance and helps soften the hard surfaces. A few larger plants screen the main drive, so the front garden can be enjoyed without having to stare at the driveway.

Figures 5.14 and 5.15.
The iron gates and free-standing wall help create the feeling of a courtyard.

TIP

A courtyard creates a soothing separation between a home's driveway and its front entrance. Use beautiful low walls or a hedge planting to create the effect.

The DelCampo front entrance is larger and more intricate than what you'd find at the average home, but the scale of the front garden compliments the size of the house. The result is not an overwhelmingly large front garden, but one that has charming appeal and creates a feeling of comfort (fig. 5.2). These are important design considerations.

The plantings. Screening and privacy were especially important design considerations for the DelCampo house, but the existing plantings on the property weren't accomplishing the tasks. Of the many trees, evergreens, and shrubs, most had been severely pruned. Several hemlocks along the front property line, for instance, had had their lower branches removed, so they provided little shielding from the busy street.

BEFORE

5.16

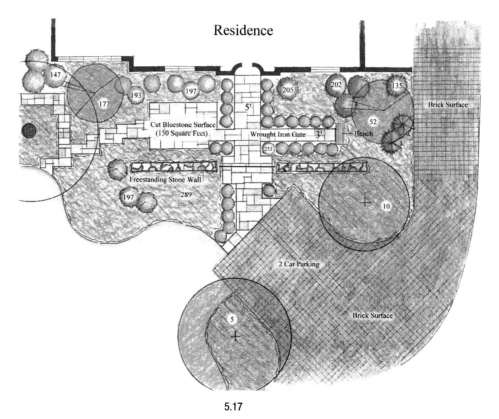

5.17

For privacy, plants were added to one side of the property to screen a large new home that was under construction and very close to the property line. An extensive plant screen was also designed along the front property line to obscure the view of traffic on the major road in front of the house. Additional hemlocks and deciduous shrubs now screen the road, create privacy, and generally improve the composition of the plants on the property. A European beech, a major shade tree, was planted near the west perimeter to soften the view of the busy street from the first and second floors.

The back garden

The DelCampos' backyard landscape required makeovers for the deck, the walk, and the plantings. The existing deck was elevated, resembling a fishing pier, and required stairs to access it. The deck railing was unsightly and blocked the view of the garden. The backyard also had many plants that were old, overgrown, and misplaced.

Figure 5.18.
The original patio, with surrounding block wall, prohibited any planting around the surface, therefore eliminating any garden feeling.

5.18

BEFORE

Figure 5.19.
The multiple seating areas are separated by new stone walls and plants but are still connected by a walk. The feeling is much more alive, warm, and inviting.

5.19

The gathering spaces. The deck was removed to make way for a series of surfaces that were interconnected and that related to the rooms within the home. Several flagstone walls were placed to create different levels for the various surfaces. The main surface was designed as a low-profile wood deck, large enough to entertain friends and family, at surface level. This deck landing was built with 2-by-4s to make the surface look more refined and to prevent buckling.

The existing wood surface directly out of the kitchen was designed to be smaller, allowing for areas of planting that soften the hard surfaces around the house and add depth and dimension to the space. This small surface, also surrounded by a flagstone retaining wall, gradually transitions into the major deck surface. Steps lead down to the area below. The result is four distinct surfaces, totaling approximately 860 sq. ft.

The walk. This unique backyard design includes a walk leading from the area outside the kitchen to the patio outside the screen porch. An existing terrace was removed to make way for the new design. A concrete block wall gave way to a beautiful flagstone retaining wall. And 10 ft. wide steps were replaced by 5 ft. flagstone steps. Along with access to the newly designed patio, also made from flagstone, this design provided better scale and more beauty for the backyard.

5.20

Figure 5.20.
A stone walk connects the two surfaces. There is ample room to plant around the surfaces to create a garden feeling.

Figure 5.21.
Additional plants were added in the back to improve privacy. The bench and flowers create additional interest.

The plantings. Softening and subtly defining the large surface areas, the plants help screen the separate areas, scale down the large surfaces, and add beauty and interest. The existing plants around the foundation were removed because they crowded the house. One of the original plantings, a 16 ft. upright Japanese yew,

5.21

BEFORE

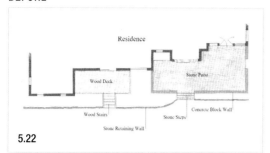

Residence

Wood Deck

Stone Patio

Wood Stairs

Stone Steps

Concrete Block Wall

Stone Retaining Wall

5.22

TIP

You and your contractor may be tempted to use 2-by-6s or 2-by-8s when designing a deck surface. After all, you might save a little money and use fewer boards. But you'll be giving up an attractive, refined look and risking the buckling that often accompanies these wider boards over time. Instead, add class and quality to your deck by sticking with 2-by-4s.

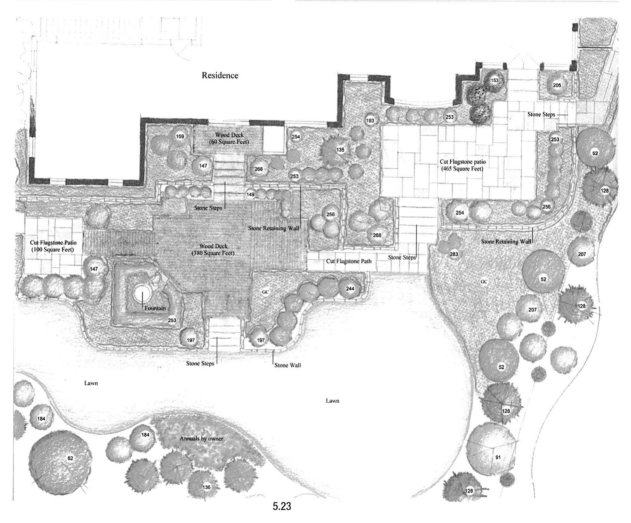

5.23

which gave some privacy to the second floor of the home, was preserved. Along the property line, an existing large spruce tree had been limbed up and provided very little screening, so it was removed. Canadian hemlocks, Douglas firs, winterberry holly, and a few small deciduous trees—including American hophornbeam—were planted to add some privacy and screening from the neighboring property.

5.24

5.25

Though it sits on 5 acres of natural beauty—woods, hills, mature trees, and a lake—some major landscaping flaws compromised the beauty of the Bilton house, which the Biltons bought from the original owners when it was three years old. The big issues: a circle drive crowded the front door of the house, and some drainage problems and a tremendous slope on one side of the property created a few trouble spots, especially in the front yard.

The front garden

To create the warm, welcoming feeling that makes a home so attractive to both its owners and its visitors, the Biltons' front garden needed a significant redesign, focusing on relocating the driveway, adding parking spaces, and defining a front garden space.

Original driveway. Despite abundant space—5 acres—on which to locate the home and the driveway, the builder forced both these major elements into one small

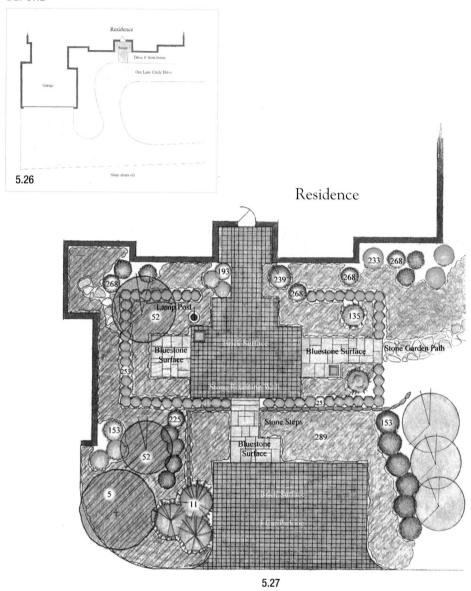

5.26

Residence

5.27

area. A circle drive came within 6 ft. of the front door and within just a few feet of a steep drop-off on the side of the property. Wedging a circle drive into such a tight spot put a lot of pavement right in front of the house. Despite all the paving, the circle drive was essentially a one-lane road, meaning there was no space for cars to get around each other. This classic case of trying to squeeze ten pounds of, er, concrete into a five pound bag made for a front entrance that was highly uncomplimentary, overly crowded, and out of scale.

New parking spaces. Although a parking area up in the yard in front of a house may not seem a very welcoming sight, in this case it was exactly what was needed to

5.28

Figure 5.28.
The retaining wall helps separate the front entrance from the parking area.

make visitors feel at home. Yes, parking spaces. In place of the circular drive, a one-lane drive with a parking area was built. The parking area gave drivers enough room to pass each other and turn around. To prevent this area from feeling like a shopping center parking lot, the edges of the parking area were softened with plants. The new driveway design not only reduced the amount of driveway surface but pulled the driveway away from the home, creating room for a front entrance garden.

Front entrance garden. With the driveway relocated, there was now space for a proper front entrance garden. A grade change created a slope that interfered with the garden space, so a stone retaining wall was built to correct the problem. The wall further benefited the landscape by creating better separation between the house and the driveway, while clearly defining the entrance garden. Four stone steps lead visitors from the drive to the front entrance. The careful design of a brick surface allows for a comfortable space to greet and bid farewell to visitors, eliminating the need to congregate on the driveway.

Plantings and other highlights. The original design of the driveway had left no space for plants at the entrance. With the new drive and the definition provided by the retaining wall, a space for planting was created. A simple planting, somewhat removed from the house to avoid a crowded look and feel, highlights the front entrance, softens the hard surfaces, and adds dimension to the yard. Existing box-

TIP

Unless you live on a large estate with an expansive front yard, skip the circular drive. It requires a lot of surface area and would quickly consume all but the largest yards.

5.29

Figure 5.29.
The original circular drive was located between the new wall and the home.

5.30

5.31

woods were relocated from the house foundation to the edge of the retaining wall and surrounding the entrance, adding depth and a sense of enclosure within the front entrance garden. Lights that once lined the driveway now highlight a quaint bluestone garden path that leads from the front entrance garden to the backyard.

The back garden

The Biltons' backyard was a victim of all-too-common run-of-the-mill contractor work, sterile and unimaginative—hardly the cozy, intimate space the Biltons envisioned for their private sanctuary. The existing patio was a large brick surface that abutted the house and ran its entire length. That left little room for plants and way too much patio surface baking in the sun. The Biltons want-

BEFORE

Residence

Brick Patio

Brick Patio

5.32

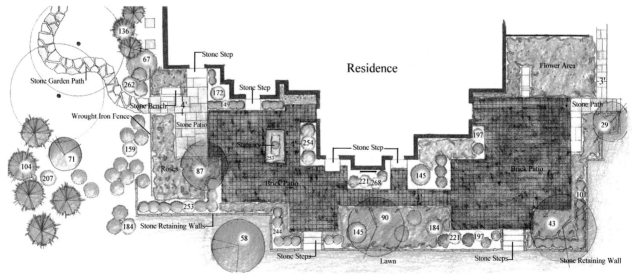

5.33

5.34

5.35

5.36

5.37

5.38

Figure 5.35 through 5.38.
The placement and plan-
ning of the planting areas
separate, and scale down
the size of, two brick patio
surfaces. Even with these
large surfaces, the garden
looks lush and beautiful.

ed a design that would let them entertain large groups and also serve as a warm space for their own private use.

Privacy and coziness. Creating an intimate space often calls for adding a plant-ing screen to the landscape. But in this 5-acre wooded setting where homes were spaced at quite a distance from each other, that wasn't an issue. The existing woods created a natural plant screen.

The backyard still lacked that warm feeling of privacy and comfort. The sterile patio crammed against the house was a case of poor design robbing a home of what could have been a naturally private and welcoming space. This property's great potential was far from maximized. The first step in this redesign was the obvious one: remove the existing patio.

Wall and hard surfaces. Along with removing the old patio, we built a low retaining wall to create a level space for several new patio surfaces. The wall also gave instant definition to the garden space, created visual interest, and separated the lawn from the garden. The newly designed patios, totaling about 1,600 sq. ft. (comparable to the original patio), are set away from the house. That allows for more interesting plantings between the house and the brick patio surfaces, while softening the hard surfaces and enveloping the space as a lush gardenlike setting.

The strategic planting helps differentiate the yard into two large, distinctly defined areas. Two sets of stone steps lead off the patios, across the lawn, and down to a lake.

The walk. Stone garden paths (figs. 5.39 and 5.40) lead from the two patio areas to the front yard. They were designed to complement the landscape. You can walk around the entire house without ever leaving a hard surface, but in no way does the property look like it's engulfed in a sea of pavement.

TIP

When working with a contractor, beware of the explanation "This is how we always do it!" Habit has often produced unimaginative landscaping but has rarely led to the right or best design solution.

A successful design. The Biltons say that the beauty of their landscape has sparked their interest in gardening. They spend more time outdoors now, and they take an active role in caring for their landscape.

– PART 2 –

Beautiful, Logical Selections

CHAPTER 6

Your Landscape

Tips for Choosing and Working with a Landscape Pro

Residential landscaping is the most intimate, intricate, and rewarding form of landscaping. Look at it this way: you spend a lot of time looking at your yard, your garden, and your property in general, so it'd better look good. The person helping you with the design must understand you—the homeowner—and your personality, your immediate and long-term goals, the pros and cons of your property, and the influence of your neighbors. And of course, to help you identify the good while steering clear of the bad and the ugly, your landscape professional needs a toolbox full of design essentials, such as solid design plans, knowledge of paving and wall materials, experience with carpentry, and familiarity with a wide variety of plants.

That's a lot for one person to deliver, and in the world of landscaping, there are two types of people who can deliver the results you desire: landscape designers and landscape architects.

Landscape designers are professionals who plan and develop landscapes at the residential or small commercial level. Landscape designers tend to be skilled in the use of plants and other horticultural aspects of landscape design. Their expertise is in making a small space look beautiful for the handful of people who care about it most—no easy task.

Landscape architects are skilled at analyzing and designing the features of the landscapes we work, live, and play in. Landscape architects are often schooled in engineering and architecture, and they typically work on larger projects than a landscape designer. Landscape architects may design parks, playgrounds, zoos, skate parks, whole residential developments, campuses, gardens, golf courses, recreation areas, and individual residential landscapes.

REFERRAL, REFERRAL, REFERRAL

Both landscape designers and landscape architects have the skills to design a beautiful, logical landscape, but selecting the one person best suited to you and your property may require something of a leap of faith. Perhaps with relatively little information, you find yourself in the position of relying on a person or a company to have your best interests in mind.

To eliminate some of the guesswork in choosing a design professional, begin as you would when choosing a plumber, an electrician, or an attorney: get a referral. It can't be emphasized enough: referral, referral, referral. As with every profession, there are stars and there are stinkers. So, ask around; talk to family, friends, colleagues, and neighbors about their garden experiences. Their stories and insights about working with landscape professionals will lead you to one with whom you can discuss his or her work experience, your yard, and hash out how the two might fit together.

Another path to finding a good landscape professional is through your own observation. When you see a garden you admire, find out who did the landscaping. Homeowners love to tell stories about their experiences, and you can gather a lot of information simply by listening to their likes and dislikes. Searching out a design professional this way takes some time, but removing as much doubt as possible about the person you choose to transform your landscape can help you preserve your sanity—and perhaps your wallet.

During your interview, take note of how well the referred landscape professional listens to you. Listening is a vital skill for both of you to make the project succeed. Also note whether there's a good exchange of ideas between the two of you. The listening and the chemistry are essential for a landscaping process that is enjoyable and meaningful.

The fun really begins when you've identified the landscape professional you'd like to work with to makeover your property. You've received a great referral, interviewed the landscape professional, and determined that there's good chemistry and a willingness to listen to each other. Now you're ready to transform your yard and garden.

As a homeowner, you may know *exactly* what you want to accomplish in your yard and even have it recorded in a written outline. Otherwise, you may just know that you want to improve something, even if you can't quite put your finger on it. It's in your best interest to know, at the least, what you feel is important for your property, what is lacking in your landscape, and what you envision as a final result of working with a landscape professional. With that in mind (and better yet, on paper), you can have a meaningful discussion about your landscaping goals. Also, by having seen the work of your landscape professional (thanks to that referral), you'll be able to talk about how his or her design process will be applied to your project.

Obviously, every homeowner is different and every property is different, but there are consistently certain questions, answers, and discussions that guide the design process. The following lists give just some of the questions that should be part of the initial design process (see earlier chapters for more questions that could be considered). Many of these questions are best addressed as you walk around your property. First survey your property on your own with these questions in mind. Then give your landscape professional a call and schedule a time to critique your property together, so you can gain a shared sense of how your ideas relate to your property, both good and bad.

What your landscape professional needs to know about your property
Both front and backyards

What problems do you have with drainage?

Does your yard create any privacy issues for you when you are inside the house?

Is privacy an issue when you are spending time in your yard?

Do you see any objectionable views as you look at your yard from inside your house?

Are there views of your yard or from indoors that you'd like to maintain or highlight?

Are there unpleasant views when you are standing in the yard?

What types of plants do you like?

Do you want flowers? Annuals or perennials?

When you've had flowers in the past, how much time have you devoted to caring for them?

Do you have pets?

Is lighting important to you? How much would you like to have?

How often do you entertain guests or family?

How many people do you entertain at a time, and what are their ages?

Front yard

Do you like the look of your front walk?

Is the front walk wide enough for guests to walk side by side and for you to stand comfortably while have a parting conversation with someone?

Is the front door visible as you approach the home?

As you walk to the front door, are you distracted by unsightly views on or off your property?

If the front door faces west, are you bothered by the afternoon sun?

Do you have children who play in your front yard?

Do you want a basketball hoop in the front yard?

If you have a side-load garage, does the existing walk take off from the drive in such a way that all you see is the garage doors (figs. 6.1 and 6.2)? Do you like this?

Backyard

Other than through the house, how do you get from the front yard to the backyard?

Which back doors do you use most to go between house and backyard?

Do you know how much surface you need for entertaining? (200 sq. ft. is small; 400 sq. ft. is large)

Are you considering a swimming pool?

Do you have another sports area requirement?

Do you want shade, privacy, or a wind screen?

Do you want to grow flowers, vegetables, fruit trees, or something else special?

Do you want a water feature?

(Left to right)
Figure 6.1.
Your existing walk might put you front and center at your garage doors.
Figure 6.2.
A simple redesign of your front walk can eliminate the direct sight line to the garage.

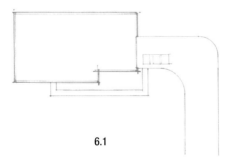
6.1

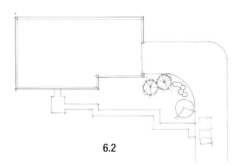
6.2

This list is by no means exhaustive, and of course, the most important questions are the ones that affect you. With an intuitive sense about what will work well for your landscape, your landscape professional should endeavor to exhaust you with questions to be sure that your preferences are foremost in the final design. Still, your task is to express yourself as fully as possible to avoid oversights.

As you go through this process of questioning and of considering your landscape, remember that your design professional is not apt to agree with everything you suggest. (In fact, there's been a time or three that we have inadvertently insulted the homeowners, and they still let us continue to help them with their properties.) Listen closely to the pro's reasoning for disagreeing with you, and ask for clarification when you need it. It's reasonable for you to expect a logical explanation when a landscape professional tells you an idea of yours won't work or, for that matter, strongly advocates any specific course of action for your property.

This whole process of questioning and discussion should also spark a comprehensive view of the project and your property. Many of the professional's questions may seem unnecessary, but be assured that this intensive process is a way for him or her to understand your thoughts, your preferences, and to hone in on the right course of action for your yard and garden, now and in the future. Remember, your landscaping is a long-term project that will develop over time, and perhaps as long as you live in your house. These early steps lead you and your landscape professional to a more thorough and carefully considered, complete design.

YOUR LANDSCAPING SOUL MATE

Is it really possible to find the "One" for you and your property, a landscaping soul mate, if you will? Well, that's the hope. You should feel confident in your relationship with each other and comfortable enough to challenge each other throughout the process of creating a new landscape for your personal space. Through thorough questioning, careful research, knowledge of your property, and creative design, your landscape professional can achieve excellent results for you.

TIP

Learning about your landscape professional's shortcomings the hard way may provide colorful stories years later, but the up-front costs can be high. Save yourself some heartache and cash by asking friends and neighbors for referrals. It's cheaper to learn from *their* mistakes.

TIP

You may be able to identify the plants at your local gas station, but that's no reason to landscape your house like one. Knowing only the usual suspects—such as spirea and burning bush—limits your ability to create a masterful composition of complementary plants.

Unless you're among the few homeowners who are well versed in the multitude of plant species on the market today, trust your landscape professional on this one. See some of your landscape professional's previous work, and if you like what you see, then trust his or her recommendations.

Still, you can also improve your plant IQ, so to speak, by taking a trip to the local nursery or arboretum. Be willing to learn!

CHAPTER 7

Garden

Admire Their Form,
Appreciate Their Function

A perfectly placed bench beckons you into a cozy corner of your garden. Garden gates welcome visitors into a friendly space. A well-tended trellis offers shade on a sunny day.

Garden structures enhance the beauty and usefulness of your garden. Such fine finishing touches as pergolas, lattice, statuary, pools, and walls complement your carefully cultivated landscape. The secret to making them enhance your yard is in finding the proper home for them. The criteria for finding that perfect home? Place every garden structure where it looks like it naturally belongs, position it so it fits seamlessly into your garden, and be sure it can be easily viewed and enjoyed.

Bench. A garden bench serves many purposes. Besides providing a place to rest, the right garden bench placed in the right spot adds architectural interest and depth to the landscape. It can be as compelling as a piece of sculpture. As with placing any sculpture, a bench should be situated among the plants so it becomes part of the

(Left to right)
Figure 7.1.
The simple design of this
bench allows it to blend in
with its surroundings.

Figure 7.2.
Place a bench among
plants so that it looks like it
belongs in the landscape.

garden composition (figs. 7.1 and 7.2). Avoid placing a bench by itself; that tends to break up the garden. Randomly sticking a bench in your yard looks like, well, it looks like you randomly stuck a bench in your yard.

When choosing the ideal spot for your bench, also take into consideration the view from the bench. When you sit and stay awhile, you'll much prefer a view of garden beauty over cars on the street.

Garden gate. Creating a separate area in the landscape is often accomplished attractively with a garden gate. A unique gate that complements the landscape will successfully draw people into another "secret" room of sorts.

The design and detail of a gate really are a prelude for what lies beyond. Plantings around the gate can soften its appearance and help it blend into the landscape. In figure 7.3, arborvitae acts as a fence, with a gate placed for access into the garden. In figures 7.4, 7.5, and 7.6, you can see how the intricate detail and classic style of a wrought iron gate gives the garden a more formal appearance. The openness of wrought iron also allows views into the garden while still separating the spaces. Figure 7.7 shows how a simple yet detailed gate signifies the entrance into a Japanese-style garden.

Figure 7.3.
This gate is an
entrance through a
"wall" of arborvitae.

7.4

7.5

7.6

(Top to bottom)

Figure 7.4.
The intricate detail of this wrought iron gate sets the stage and creates intrigue as you enter this large estate.

Figure 7.5.
Wrought iron paired with brick creates a very formal appearance.

Figure 7.6.
Wrought iron gates and fences not only are beautiful but allow views in and out of the property, while still creating separation.

Figure 7.7.
The simple design of this gate complements the Japanese garden inside.

7.7

Lattice or trellis. When constructed and placed appropriately in the landscape, lattice can create an elegant screen. Intersperse plantings with the lattice structure to soften its appearance and avoid the look of a solid, confining screen (fig. 7.8). Lattice is also an excellent structure for growing vines and groundcover.

Figure 7.8.
Incorporate plantings with lattice to avoid a "great wall" appearance.

Pergola or arbor. Giving a beautiful framework to your garden, a pergola or arbor creates an extra level of dimension and interest. A pergola is a garden structure consisting of regularly spaced columns, flat roof, and and open wooden framework, sometimes latticed. It is made to support climbing or vining plants, which cover the structure. A pergola is often placed over a walk or patio for shade. An arbor is similar in that it supports climbing and vining plants. An arbor is smaller than a pergola and often has an arched roof. Oftentimes an arbor is placed over a small bench. A pergola or arbor is also often incorporated as an open gate into a garden area (figs. 7.9 and 7.10). Choosing a structure that is appropriate is essential to the development of your landscape as a composition. Pergola designs can be either formal or informal, so you can easily complement a particularly well-appointed landscape or a more relaxed one.

Be sure to use the pergola with purpose, such as providing shade or privacy. Otherwise, you risk that disjointed feeling of having added something that doesn't really belong.

Statuary. Garden statues can add personality and interest to your space, especially when they're part of an eye-pleasing, unified composition. Statuary looks best when it's carefully incorporated into the garden, when it looks as though it truly belongs. In figure 7.11 statuary is ideally situated among plants. Figure 7.12 shows a great example of placing statuary near a pool framed by plants.

(Above) Figure 7.11.
This bold statue is put on display by a pool surrounded by plants.

(Left) Figure 7.12.
This interesting sculpture, tucked in among plants, is a nice surprise in the garden.

Art pieces are meant to be viewed and enjoyed while in the garden or while looking out your window into it. Figure 7.13 depicts how just a slight creative alteration can make a world of difference in the appeal of garden statuary: the birdbath was removed from its pedestal and placed among the pachysandra, almost at ground level. This creates a much nicer composition, with the birdbath nestling in the groundcover.

Freestanding wall. Adding a unique sculptural element to a garden, a freestanding wall can beautifully divide a large space into smaller, cozy spaces. Designed and placed appropriately, a freestanding wall adds depth and interest to the garden.

Pool or pond. The point can't be made often enough: Ponds, pools, and other water features are a big responsibility (cleaning, pumps, filters, winterization, and more). If you're up for the work, though, you should make the most of the beauty of your pool or pond. To do that, incorporate the pool or pond into a landscape space where it will look natural. For instance, avoid placing a waterfall in a naturally flat area. We've all seen it done: on a flat piece of ground, a waterfall built up, using soil and usually a massive amount of stone or boulders. However, this looks very unnatural and odd. Also, every water feature needs a backdrop, and one is usually created with plants.

If a garden area cannot support a pool or a pond in a natural-looking way, consider a water feature that is more architectural in form, such as a rectangle. Obviously, a rectangular water feature is not natural, and that's the point—you're making it a more formal feature. Another approach would be to incorporate a fountain in the same manner that you would a piece of statuary.

Pools are generally large and can dominate a yard. To make the most of them visually, in-ground pools are preferred over aboveground pools, since the walls of aboveground pools will never blend into a landscape. Use plants, natural pavers, and perhaps a water feature—such as a waterfall at one end of the in-ground pool—to make it an attractive part of the yard.

Lawn ornament. And finally, the garden structure we love to hate. Lawn ornament has become an unfortunate American standard. Gazing balls, the over-dressed cement goose, fake deer, gnomes, replicas of the Statue of Liberty, and so on, each one just as hideous as the next. If you deem one of these necessary for your garden, please, please place it in the backyard. This way you can enjoy your prized "art" piece from your patio and window—without imposing your personal taste on the unsuspecting passerby. Beauty is, after all, in the eye of the homeowner.

Figure 7.15.
Nestled among a backdrop of plants, this fountain is a highlight in the garden.

CHAPTER 8

Beautiful,

Recommendations for Home Landscapes

Beautiful, healthy plants create a beautiful, compelling landscape. As homeowners, we tend to know only a few plants—namely, those that are prevalent in our neighborhoods. This chapter is intended to be a guide, giving you options and inspiring ideas as you decide which plants—from specimen trees to hedges, from shrubs to groundcovers—to place in your yard and garden. It is not important that you choose the exact ones—not a particular variety or even species, necessarily—that are recommended here. You should, however, choose plants that are at least similar in size, shape, texture, and function to the recommendations.

There are many considerations in choosing the right plants for your property, such as geographical hardiness zone, space available in your landscape, and other plants already on your property. Plant variety characteristics to consider include whether a plant is deciduous or evergreen, its ultimate size, and its pruning tolerance.

Some plants, for instance, can be pruned very nicely to stay at a height somewhat less than their natural, full-grown size. Others can't, and knowing which are which can make all the difference in the beauty of your yard.

This chapter's recommendations don't cover every hardiness zone for every plant category. Your local nursery, garden center, horticultural supply company, arboretum, or garden club can help you make a zone-specific selection that is comparable to a variety recommended here. So, if there's a deciduous plant that's recommended in this chapter but doesn't grow in your planting zone, you might instead end up choosing a broadleaf evergreen that shares many of the other plant's desirable characteristics but is right for your location.

Plant numbers in this chapter correspond to the numbers in the landscape plans.

SHADE TREES: 40 FEET AND LARGER

Shade trees are the major plant components of the landscape. As the term implies, these large trees provide shade and relief. Base your choice of either a multiple-stem or single-stem variety on where you want to place it in your landscape. A multiple-stem shade tree adds beautiful structure and screening to an area, whereas a single-stem tree allows you to look beyond and enjoy the view.

1. *Acer rubrum*, red maple
   Height 40–60 ft., Zones 3–9
   Leaves emerge with a red tint, then change to green or dark green. Excellent fall color, ranging from yellow to bright red. The tree has a pyramidal habit when it's young, changing to rounded or irregular with age. Good lawn or park tree.

2. *Acer rubrum* 'October Glory', 'October Glory' maple
   Height 40–50 ft., Zones 3–9
   Oval habit. Its fall color ranges from brilliant orange to red.

3. *Acer rubrum* 'Red Sunset', 'Red Sunset' maple
   Height 45–50 ft., Zones 3–9
   This excellent tree has attractive foliage with gorgeous red fall color. Top-notch cultivar with a nice pyramidal to broad, rounded habit. Does well in cold climates.

4. *Acer* x *freemanii* 'Autumn Blaze', 'Autumn Blaze' maple
   Height 50 ft., Zones 3–9
   Silver and red maple hybrid. This adaptable shade tree has a fast growth rate, an upright habit, and excellent red to orange fall color.

Acer saccharum

5. *Acer saccharum*, sugar maple
   Height 60 ft., Zones 4–8
   Best of the large shade trees, with excellent fall color. It suffers from extended heat, though, so it's best for cooler zones.

6. *Carpinus betulus*, European hornbeam
   Height 40–60 ft., Zones 4–7
   Beautiful smooth, gray bark. There are light green flower bracts and catkins in April, which will produce nuts that ripen in September. The dark green leaves of summer turn yellow in late fall. It is tolerant of most soil conditions but prefers well-drained soil. Also prefers full sun.

7. *Celtis occidentalis*, hackberry
   Height 50 ft., Zones 3–9
   Happy in tough conditions, soil, and wind.

8. *Celtis occidentalis* 'Chicagoland', 'Chicagoland' hackberry
   Height 50 ft., Zones 3–9
   Similar to species but develops a single leader.

9. *Fagus grandiflora*, American beech
   Height 60 ft., Zones 4–9
   This beautiful native tree grows in the many wooded areas of northern Indiana and southern Michigan. It offers interest in all seasons, with attractive dark green leaves, golden bronze fall color, and smooth, blue-gray bark. It tends to be a low-branched tree. This species is more tolerant of adverse conditions than European beech, *F. sylvatica*, and outgrows it, as well. One of the best ornamental trees: strong, tolerant, interesting year-round, and long-lived.

10. *Fagus sylvatica*, European beech
    Height 50 ft., Zones 4–7
    An overwhelmingly beautiful tree, with attractive structure, smooth, gray bark, and lustrous, dark green leaves. Its branching begins close to the ground. Best for cooler zones.

Fagus sylvatica

11. *Fagus sylvatica* 'Purpurea', purple European beech
    Height 60–90 ft., Zones 4–7
    This large, ornamental shade tree has attractive purple foliage that fades to purple-tinged green.

Fagus sylvatica 'Purpurea'

12. *Fraxinus americana* 'Autumn Purple', purple ash
    Height 50 ft., Zones 4–9
    Glossy leaves and good purple fall color.

13. *Fraxinus pensylvanica* 'Patmore', 'Patmore' green ash
    Height 50 ft., Zones 3–8
    Uniform growing habit. Its glossy leaves have yellow fall color.

14. *Ginkgo biloba*, ginkgo
    Height 50 ft., Zones 4–8
    Unusual habit and distinctive fan-shaped leaves. Golden yellow fall color. The leaves may not turn yellow in colder climates, though, and if there's an early frost, green leaves may all fall within twenty-four hours. Dependable in warmer zones.

15. *Gleditsia triacanthos* var. *inermis*, thornless common honey locust
    Height 30–70 ft., Zones 4–9
    Open habit. Fragrant flowers May to June. The small compound leaves have yellow fall color.

16. *Gleditsia triacanthos* var. *inermis* 'Skyline', 'Skyline' honey locust
    Height 45 ft., Zones 4–9
    One of the best honey locust cultivars. The dark green compound leaves change to a bright golden yellow in fall.

17. *Gymnocladus dioicus*, Kentucky coffeetree
    Height 60–70 ft., Zones 3–8
    Interesting branching habit with compound leaves. This tree has attractive bark and leathery, reddish brown pods. It's ideal for a large area, and there are several good cultivars to choose from.

18. *Larix deciduas*, European larch
    Height 50–75 ft., Zones 3–6
    Tall, cone-bearing deciduous tree—a conifer that's not an evergreen. The bright green leaf color of spring turns ochre yellow in the fall; either color is spectacular. A charming tree with an attractive structure, it does require a large area to grow in.

19. *Larix kaempferi*, Japanese larch
    Height 70–90 ft., Zones 4–7
    Fast-growing deciduous conifer. The fine green foliage turns yellow-gold in the fall. Plant in a sunny location because this tree won't tolerate shade.

20. *Liquidambar styraciflua*, American sweetgum

    Height 60 ft., Zones 5–9

    The star-shaped leaves provide excellent fall color. In Zone 5 be sure to plant this tree in a well-protected area. Moist sites are ideal. The fruit is a bit messy as spiky, dry "gumballs" on the ground, but it can be interesting while persisting on the branches.

21. *Liriodendron tulipifera*, tulip tree

    Height 70–90 ft., Zones 4–9

    An unusual and attractive tree with tuliplike flowers May to June. It is best suited to larger properties. Specimens grown in Zone 4 will be smaller than those in warmer zones.

22. *Magnolia acuminata*, cucumbertree magnolia

    Height 50–80 ft., Zones 4–8

    A large, beautiful, open tree with dark green leaves. The young tree's pyramidal habit becomes broad and rounded with age. The slightly fragrant, greenish to yellow flowers bloom May to June; they're not very showy. The massive, spreading branches are suited to a large open space.

23. *Metasequoia glyptostroboides*, dawn redwood

    Height 100 ft., Zones 4–8

    This is an extremely fast-growing deciduous conifer. Its soft, bright, green foliage turns bronze in fall.

24. *Phellodendron amurense*, Amur corktree

    Height 30–45 ft., Zones 3–7

    A broad, spreading habit makes this tree wider (50 ft.) than it is tall (30–45 ft.). Its compound leaves are lustrous green, changing to bronze or yellow in the fall. The older tree has interesting, attractive, corklike bark.

25. *Platanus* x *acerifolia*, London planetree

    Height 70–100 ft., Zones 4–9

    This large shade tree has a very large crown; interesting olive green and white, exfoliating bark; and large, glossy green leaves. It prefers warm summer conditions.

26. *Quercus alba*, white oak

    Height 50 ft., Zones 3–9

    The state tree of Illinois is the most handsome of the oaks. Dark green leaves in summer.

27. *Quercus bicolor*, swamp white oak

Height 75–100 ft., Zones 4–8

This large shade tree with a large canopy is one of the fastest-growing oaks. It prefers moist areas and transplants easily.

28. *Quercus coccinea*, scarlet oak

Height 70–75 ft., Zones 4–9

Excellent scarlet red fall color. The pyramidal habit of this tree's youth changes to a round, open habit with age.

29. *Quercus imbricaria*, shingle oak

Height 50 ft., Zones 4–8

The leaves are reddish as they unfold, changing to a dark green in the summer. In fall the leaves turn yellow-brown to russet red, and they persist through the winter. A lovely oak tree.

30. *Quercus macrocarpa*, burr oak

Height 70–80 ft., Zones 3–8

This large shade tree's acorns have fuzzy, "burred" caps. Among oak trees this one is the most tolerant of urban conditions.

31. *Quercus palustris*, pin oak

Height 60–70 ft., Zones 4–8

A common landscape oak, with an interesting pyramidal habit that makes it a good lawn or street tree. The dark green leaves turn bronze-red in fall.

32. *Quercus prinus*, chestnut oak

Height 60–70 ft., Zones 4–8

Lustrous, dark yellow-green leaves change to an orangey yellow in fall. It has rich, dark brown bark and dark brown acorns. Tolerates poor soil conditions.

33. *Quercus rubra*, red oak

Height 60–75 ft., Zones 4–7

This valuable, fast-growing oak needs full sun. The foliage changes from dark green to russet-red in fall, then to bright red.

34. *Sophora japonica*, Japanese pagodatree

Height 50–75 ft., Zones 4–7

This tree's excellent flowers and good foliage are its principal assets. Lustrous, bright- to medium-green leaf color in summer. Wide, creamy white, 6 to 12 in. long flower panicles bloom from July to mid-August. It has a broadly rounded crown at maturity and is a good tree for city conditions.

35. *Taxodium distichum*, bald cypress
Height 50 ft., Zones 4–11
This deciduous conifer with a pyramidal habit becomes 20 to 30 ft. wide. Attractive bark. Its needle-like leaves are bright yellow-green in spring, green in summer, orange-brown in fall. It grows in or out of water. Interesting nutlike fruit.

36. *Taxodium distichum* 'Apache Chief', 'Apache Chief' bald cypress
Height 50 ft., Zones 4–11
Similar to the species but wider and more attractive.

37. *Tilia americana*, American linden
Height 100 ft., Zones 3–9
This long-living, large shade tree is heavy blooming, with fragrant, pale yellow flowers in spring.

38. *Tilia cordata*, littleleaf linden
Height 50 ft., Zones 3–7
Excellent tree for uniformity and quality.

39. *Tilia tomentosa*, silver linden
Height 50–70 ft., Zones 4–7
This fabulous shade tree with a pyramidal habit is easy to grow as a multiple-stem tree. Its leaves are lustrous and dark green on top, with silvery undersides. Fragrant, yellowish white flowers. An excellent street tree. Tolerant to drought.

40. *Zelkova serrata*, Japanese Zelkova
Height 50–80 ft., Zones 5–8
This very handsome tree has an interesting vase-shaped habit. Its foliage—dark green in the summer—and bark are especially attractive.

SMALL DECIDUOUS TREES: 15 TO 40 FEET

Small trees, commonly referred to as ornamental trees when in the home landscape, have distinctive, showy characteristics, such as flowers, berries, unusual bark, or unique structure. Such a tree is meant to be seen, whether up close, like from a patio or front walk, or from a distance. Place it in a spot where it can be enjoyed.

Ornamentals are grown and available as either multiple- or single-stem trees. Don't skimp! Seek out the unrivaled, truly superior multiple-stem plant.

41. *Acer campestre*, hedge maple
Height 25–35 ft., Zones 4–8
Small, dark green leaves. Good for a difficult location, such as dry or poor soil or air pollution. It tolerates abuse and adapts well. Use where there may be height restrictions, such as around power lines.

42. *Acer circinatum*, Oregon vine maple
    Height 10–25 ft., Zones 5–6
    With a compact structure, this maple is used in landscape screens as a small tree or large shrub. The flower clusters vary from white to purple. Foliage has yellow-orange fall color.

43. *Acer ginnala*, Amur maple
    Height 15–25 ft., Zones 3–8
    Best in Zones 3–6. The small, glossy leaves develop excellent fall color.

Acer ginnala

44. *Acer ginnala* 'Embers', 'Embers' Amur maple
    Height 15–20 ft., Zones 3–8
    This spreading form of Amur maple has attractive bright red samaras (fruit) and excellent fall color.

45. *Acer griseum*, paperbark maple
    Height 20–30 ft., Zones 5–6
    Supreme beauty in exfoliating bark and structure. Reddish fall color.

46. *Acer palmatum*, Japanese maple
    Height 15–25 ft., Zones 5–8
    Excellent yellow-bronze, dark red, orange, or purple color in the fall.

47. *Acer palmatum* 'Atropurpureum', red leaf Japanese maple
Height 15–20 ft., Zones 5–8
Red-leaved cultivar of Japanese maple.

48. *Acer pensylvanicum*, snakebark maple
Height 15–20 ft., Zones 3–7
This maple is named for its attractive smooth, green-and-white-striped bark, which turns reddish in winter. Excellent yellow fall foliage color. The tree has a shrublike appearance, likes partial shade, and tolerates moisture.

49. *Acer tataricum*, Tatarian maple
Height 30 ft., Zones 3–8
A large shrub or small tree with attractive bright-red samaras. Fall foliage varies from red to yellow.

50. *Alnus glutinosa*, European alder
Height 40 ft., Zones 4–7
Featuring attractive catkins, this tree prefers moist soil and either sun or partial shade. Best as a multiple-stemmed tree.

51. *Amelanchier canadensis*, shadblow serviceberry
Height 25 ft., Zones 3–7
Small, ornamental tree with white flowers in early spring. Edible red berries turn black as they continue to ripen late in the spring or early summer. The foliage has good yellow, orange, or red fall color.

52. *Amelanchier* x *grandiflora*, apple serviceberry
Height 20 ft., Zones 4–9
Grows in sun or partial shade. Pink buds in late April or early May precede white flowers. Red to purple berries. Excellent fall foliage color.

Amelanchier x *grandiflora*

53. *Amelanchier* x *grandiflora* 'Robin Hill', 'Robin Hill' apple serviceberry
Height 30 ft., Zones 4–9
Dark pink flower buds open to light pink flowers, fading to white, resulting in edible fruit. Excellent fall color, ranging from yellow to red. Grown as a multi-stemmed tree.

54. *Betula nigra* 'Heritage', 'Heritage' birch
Height 40 ft., Zones 3–8
This superior cultivar, with glossy leaves and exfoliating bark, does well in either a wet or a dry environment.

55. *Caragana arborescens*, Siberian peashrub
Height 15–20 ft., Zones 2–7
This vigorous shrub with compound leaves is excellent in screening or a wind-break. It is also a good plant for poor growing conditions. Yellow flowers bloom in mid-May.

56. *Carpinus caroliniana*, blue beech
Height 20 ft., Zones 4–9
Multiple-stemmed tree that can be used in naturalizing areas. Avoid spaces that are open and windswept. Handsome appearance, structure, and bark.

57. *Cercidiphyllum japonicum*, Katsura tree
Height 40 ft., Zones 4–8
Attractive leaves emerge a beautiful reddish color, changing in fall to apricot orange. Everything about this tree is beautiful—even the leaf petioles.

Cercidiphyllum japonicum

58. *Cercis canadensis*, eastern redbud
Height 20 ft., Zones 4–9
One of the most reliable spring-blooming small trees, it bursts with rosy pink flowers in March and April. Numerous cultivars. Full sun or light shade.

Cercis canadensis

59. ***Chionanthus retusus**, Chinese fringetree*

Height 15–25 ft., Zones 6–8

This large ornamental shrub or small tree has abundant white flowers in summer, then dark blue fruit. The leaves are an attractive dark green on top, downy white underneath. This tree tolerates alkaline soil.

60. ***Chionanthus virginicus**, white fringetree*

Height 12–18 ft., Zones 4–9

A large ornamental shrub or small tree, it is late to leaf out, in mid to late May. Fragrant, 6 to 7 in. white panicles flower in mid-May, followed by blue berries. Quite handsome, it likes full sun to light shade.

61. ***Cladrastis kentukea**, yellowwood*

Height 30 ft., Zones 4–8

One of the most beautiful flowering trees, this one has white, fragrant flowers in June and beechlike bark.

62. ***Cornus alternifolia**, pagoda dogwood*

Height 15 ft., Zones 3–7

Yellowish white flowers bloom in May to early June. This tree also features horizontal branching, blue berries, and good fall color.

63. ***Cornus florida**, flowering dogwood*

Cornus alternifolia

Height 25 ft., Zones 5–9

Spectacular in the higher zones. White bracts flower in April. This tree's fruit, fall color, and horizontal branching are outstanding.

64. ***Cornus kousa**, kousa dogwood*

Height 20 ft., Zones 5–8

Vase shaped when young, this dogwood becomes horizontally branched when older. Bracts are whitish to pink in May. The dark green leaves change to a scarlet fall color. The fruit complements the tree as one of many interesting characteristics.

Cornus kousa

65. *Cornus kousa* var. *chinensis*, Chinese kousa dogwood
Height 20–30 ft., Zones 5–8
A large shrub or small tree that prefers sun or partial shade. It has a wide, spreading habit and attractive white flowers (larger than those of the species), followed by edible red fruit.

66. *Cornus macrophylla*, bigleaf dogwood
Height 35 ft., Zones 5–7
Yellowish white flower panicles are 4–6 in. across and bloom in July and August. Tolerant of dry soils. Prefers full sun to partial shade.

67. *Cornus mas*, Cornelian cherry dogwood
Height 20 ft., Zones 4–7
Small, multiple-stem tree with attractive leaves, fall color, and berries. The flowers are yellow and bloom before the leaves flourish in April. Force early bloom by bringing branches with flower buds indoors in spring.

68. *Cornus officianalis*, Japanese cherry dogwood
Height 20 ft., Zones 5–8
This ornamental's yellow flowers are more spectacular and even earlier blooming than those of *Cornus mas*. The interesting bark is gray, brown, and orange.

69. *Corylus avellana*, European filbert
Height 12–20 ft., Zones 4–8
Nice, small tree with edible nuts.

70. *Crataegus crus-galli*, cockspur hawthorn
Height 20 ft., Zones 4–6
A wide-spreading hawthorn with dense, horizontal branches—a handsome structure. The leaves are a lustrous, dark green, turning bronze-red in fall. White flowers are followed by red fruit. The thornless variety (*Crataegus crusgalli* var. *inermis*) is the better purchase.

71. *Crataegus phaenopyrum*, Washington hawthorn
Height 25 ft., Zones 4–7
White flowers, excellent fall color, and colorful red fruit.

72. *Crataegus viridis*, green hawthorn
Height 35 ft., Zones 4–7
Attractive glossy green leaves and exfoliating silver-gray bark are key ornamental features. White flowers bloom in spring, and the bright red fruit persist into winter. This hawthorn is particularly drought tolerant.

73. *Euonymus europaeus*, European euonymus
Height 12–25 ft., Zones 4–7
Flowers are attractive but not showy. The pink-red fruit opens to expose orange seeds. The fruit provides a striking contrast when next to upright evergreens.

74. *Euonymus europaeus* 'Aldenhamensis', 'Aldenhamensis' European euonymus
Height 12–25 ft., Zones 4–7
Compared to the species, this is much more profusely fruiting, and the branches are more pendulous.

75. *Halesia tetraptera*, Carolina silverbell
Height 25 ft., Zones 4–7
A low-branched tree good for a shrub border. The bell-shaped, white to pale rose flower blooms from April to early May. Best in shade.

76. *Heptacodium miconioides*, seven sons tree
Height 6–8 ft., Zones 5–8
Best used in a border, this arching ornamental displays interesting flowers, fruit, and foliage.

77. *Koelreuteria paniculata*, golden rain tree
Height 30 ft., Zones 5–8
This attractive, dense tree has spectacular yellow flowers in July.

78. *Laburnum alpinum*, Scotch laburnum
Height 30 ft., Zones 4–7
A small tree or large shrub with an upright habit. The very attractive yellow flowers are borne on 16 in. racemes in May.

79. *Lagerstroemia indica*, common crapemyrtle
Height 15–20 ft., Zones 6–9
Can be used as either a shrub or a tree, but it will require pruning to improve its overall architectural appearance. The flowers vary in color from white, pinkish purple, or deep red in July.

80. *Magnolia denudata*, Yulan magnolia

Height 30–40 ft., Zones 5–8

This tree features a broad pyramidal habit. The showy, fragrant, 5 to 6 in., cup-shaped, white to ivory flowers of the species have nine to twelve petals. The flowers open early during a warm spell and can be damaged by later frost. There are many cultivars, with flower colors ranging from light pink to almost purple.

81. *Magnolia* x *soulangiana*, saucer magnolia

Height 20–25 ft., Zones 4–9

The white, pink, to purple flowers bloom in March to April. The foliage is bold. This magnolia should be planted as a lawn tree.

82. *Magnolia stellata*, star magnolia

Height 20 ft., Zones 4–8

Fragrant, star-shaped, white flowers appear before the leaves in March to April. This tree makes a striking structure plant in shaded areas as its interesting open branching develops.

83. *Malus* 'Beverly', 'Beverly' crabapple

Height 15–25 ft., Zones 4–7

The red buds open to single white flowers, followed by excellent bright-red fruit.

84. *Malus* 'Donald Wyman', 'Donald Wyman' crabapple

Height 20 ft., Zones 4–7

Wide-spreading tree 20 ft. high by 25 ft. wide. Lustrous, dark green foliage. Red to pink flower buds open to white in April. Glossy, bright-red fruit. This crabapple has an attractive structure and makes an excellent choice.

85. *Malus floribunda*, Japanese flowering crabapple

Height 15–25 ft. Zones 4–7

The deep pink to red buds become beautiful flowers that fade to white when open. The fruit is yellow. The tree has a broad, rounded habit and dark green leaves. We highly recommend this crabapple.

86. *Malus hupehensis*, tea flowering crabapple

Height 20–25 ft. Zones 4–7

The fragrant, deep pink flower buds fade to white when open. The fruit changes from greenish yellow to red. This crabapple also has a picturesque vase-shaped structure.

87. *Malus* 'Prairifire', 'Prairifire' crabapple
Height 20 ft. Zones 4–7
Red buds open to dark, purple-red flowers. Dark red to purple fruit. The upright habit of the young tree changes to a more rounded habit with age.

88. *Malus* 'Snowdrift', 'Snowdrift' flowering crabapple
Height 20 ft., Zones 4–7
Buds are pink and open to white, followed by orange-red fruit. This crab has a dense, rounded habit; is a vigorous grower; and features lustrous, dark green foliage.

89. *Malus* 'White Angel', 'White Angel' crabapple
Height 20 ft., Zones 4–7
Its pink buds open to pure-white, single flowers 1 in. in diameter. The tree also has glossy red fruit and lustrous, dark green foliage. It grows 20 ft. high and wide.

90. *Nyssa sylvatica*, black gum
Height 30 ft., Zones 4–9
One of the best native trees, it has an interesting structure, with horizontal branching. Dark green foliage emerges in the spring. The excellent fall color ranges from brilliant yellow to orange to scarlet to purple.

91. *Ostrya virginiana*, American hophornbeam
Height 20 ft., Zones 3–9
This pyramidal tree has dark green leaves that change to a yellow fall color. It's an attractive, sturdy native tree for full sun or partial shade.

92. *Oxydendrum arboreum*, sourwood
Height 20 ft., Zones 3–9
Pyramidal tree with drooping branches—an attractive form. Rich green in spring, becoming lustrous, dark green, then in fall yellow, red, then purple. White flowers bloom in late June. This is an excellent flowering tree, one of the best.

93. *Parrotia persica*, Persian ironwood
Height 25 ft., Zones 4–8
This tree grows as a multiple-stem plant. The leaves—reddish purple as they unfold, changing to lustrous, dark green—are this tree's best feature. Fall color is yellow to orange-scarlet. The older tree develops attractive exfoliating bark.

94. *Ptelea trifoliata*, hoptree
Height 15–20 ft., Zones 3–9
This large shrub or small tree bears small, fragrant, white flowers in May to June. An interesting native plant, it grows well in either sun or shade.

95. *Rhus typhina*, staghorn sumac

Height 15–25 ft., Zones 4–8

The bright green foliage of summer changes to yellow, orange, then scarlet in fall—quite spectacular. Crimson fruit persists from late August through April. A naturalizing plant. Cultivar 'Laciniata' has deeply divided leaves with a fernlike appearance.

96. *Sassafras albidum*, sassafras

Height 30 ft., Zones 4–9

It has a pyramidal shape, eventually, but an irregular shape in youth. This is a handsome tree in terms of bark, branches, and blue fruit. It is ideal for naturalizing your landscape, as it complements natural areas like woods. Its fall color is one of the best, ranging from yellow to deep orange to scarlet to purple.

97. *Styrax japonicus*, Japanese snowball

Height 20 ft., Zones 5–8

Plant this lovely low, horizontal-branching tree in a protected area. It has handsome variable gray bark. The white, bell-shaped flowers, May to June, are beautiful and slightly fragrant. The attractive leaves are yellowish red in fall if there isn't an early frost. This is a beautiful tree to be used and enjoyed in your outdoor living area or wherever else it can be viewed from indoors and out.

98. *Syringa pekinensis*, Peking lilac

Height 15–20 ft., Zones 4–7

This small, ornamental tree bears dense, creamy white flower panicles. Very handsome exfoliating, golden-brown bark.

99. *Syringa reticulata*, Japanese tree lilac

Height 25 ft., Zones 3–7

This large shrub or small tree makes an excellent sun-loving specimen. Its flowers are perfect, creamy white, and fragrant, blooming in early to mid-June. It's the least troublesome lilac.

100. *Syringa reticulata* 'Ivory Silk', ivory silk Japanese tree lilac

Height 20–25 ft., Zones 3–7

Heavy flowering, deep green leaves, compact, rounded form.

101. *Viburnum sieboldii*, Siebold viburnum

Height 15–20 ft., Zones 4–7

Excellent foliage, flowers, and fruit. The leaves are lustrous and dark green. The creamy white flowers bloom in late May. The fruit is rose-red to red, changing to black and lasting a couple of weeks.

Offering year-round green foliage in a range of textures, large evergreens are most commonly used to screen objectionable views and provide color in the landscape.

102. *Abies alba*, European silver fir

Height 160 ft., Zones 4–6

Its lustrous, dark green needles have two distinct, silvery white bands underneath.

103. *Abies balsamea*, balsam fir

Height 75 ft., Zones 3–5

This popular Christmas tree performs best in cold climates and prefers moist, acidic soil.

104. *Abies concolor*, concolor fir

Height 120 ft., Zones 4–7

This background plant has a pyramidal form and soft needles that make excellent blue-gray foliage.

105. *Abies fraseri*, Fraser fir

Height 40 ft., Zones 4–7

This is a very elegant, slow-growing evergreen with compact structure. It is also one of the best choices of Christmas tree.

106. *Abies lasiocarpa* var. *arizonica*, corkbark fir

Height 40 ft., Zones 5–6

Named for its corky, white bark, this fir has a dense, pyramidal habit and attractive blue-green to blue-white needles.

Abies concolor

107. *Cedrus atlantica*, Atlas cedar

Height 60 ft., Zones 6–9

This is a beautiful specimen tree. It has a pyramidal habit and gray-green needles. Heat and drought tolerant.

108. *Chamaecyparis lawsoniana*, Port Orford cedar

Height 60 ft., Zones 5–7

Its bluish green foliage is dense, soft, and very graceful. The tree has a pyramidal habit.

109. *Chamaecyparis obtusa*, Japanese falsecypress

Height 50–70 ft., Zones 5–8

This slow-growing specimen tree has dark green foliage.

110. *Chamaecyparis pisifera*, Japanese falsecypress

Height 50–70 ft., Zones 4–8

A pyramidal conifer. The dark green, flattened, feathery leaves are very attractive. Very small cones. The handsome smooth, reddish brown bark peels off in strips. Many cultivars are available and are distinguished by foliage type: normal, similar to the species; filifera, bearing stringy, threadlike leaves; plumosa, similar to the species, but the leaves are more open and fernlike; and squarrosa, with irregular, fluffy foliage that feels very soft, like a stuffed animal.

111. *Juniperus chinensis* 'Fairview', 'Fairview' juniper

Height 20 ft., Zones 4–9

This tree with a narrow pyramidal habit (10 ft. wide) grows vigorously, performing best in the sun. The bright green foliage is excellent in the winter. The tree produces pea-size, silver-gray berries.

Juniperus chinensis 'Fairview'

112. *Juniperus virginiana* 'Canaertii', Canaert juniper

Height 20 ft., Zones 3–9

Beautiful, dark green foliage. This juniper has attractive small, gray-blue fruit that is pungent. With a pyramidal form, it performs best in the sun.

113. *Picea abies*, Norway spruce

Height 50 ft., Zones 3–7

This fast-growing evergreen has a pyramidal form and dark green foliage. Excellent in an open, windswept location, it prefers a cold climate.

114. *Picea breweriana*, Brewer's spruce

Height 100 ft., Zone 5

This decorative specimen tree is pyramidal in youth, but its branches become pendulous with age. Attractive dark blue to green needles.

115. *Picea engelmannii*, Engelmann spruce

Height 40–50 ft., Zones 3–5

This spruce has attractive light bluish needles and a pyramidal habit.

116. *Picea glauca*, white spruce

Height 40–60 ft., Zones 2–6

Its pendulous branches create interest and bear silver to green needles. This spruce is tolerant of wind and wet soil.

117. *Picea glauca* 'Densata', Black Hills spruce

Height 20–40 ft., Zones 2–6

Slow growing and compact, this evergreen is particularly hardy and has bluish green needles.

118. *Picea omorika*, Serbian spruce

Height 50–60 ft., Zones 4–7

Here's an accent plant with graceful drooping branches in a narrow, pyramidal habit. It does not perform well in a windbreak.

119. *Picea orientalis*, Oriental spruce

Height 50 ft., Zones 4–7

A dense, narrow, pyramidal evergreen with attractive lustrous, dark green needles and an interesting horizontal branching pattern, this makes a handsome specimen in the landscape.

120. *Picea pungens*, Colorado spruce

Height 30–60 ft., Zones 3–7

Gray-green to blue-green foliage.

121. *Picea pungens* var. *glauca*, Colorado blue spruce

Height 30–60 ft., Zones 3–7

This spruce is known for its bluish needles.

122. *Picea pungens* 'Hoopsi', 'Hoopsi' blue spruce

Height 30–60 ft., Zones 3–7

One of the bluest spruces, it has a stiff, layered branching structure in a broad, pyramidal habit.

123. *Pinus aristata*, bristlecone pine

Height 8–20 ft., Zones 4–7

This slow-growing, compact dwarf pine has a picturesque habit.

124. *Pinus cembra*, Swiss stone pine

Height 30–40 ft., Zones 3–7

A narrow pyramid in youth, this slow grower becomes spreading, open, and flat topped at maturity. Attractive needles also help make it picturesque.

125. *Pinus densiflora* 'Umbraculifera', Tanyosho pine

Height 20 ft., Zones 4–7

Grown as a multiple-stem tree, it can be quite the specimen to have in your garden, with orange-red bark and soft needles.

126. *Pinus flexilis*, limber pine

Height 25 ft., Zones 4–7

This is a very attractive specimen with structural interest and bluish green needles.

127. *Pinus parviflora*, Japanese white pine

Height 25–50 ft., Zones 4–7

The crown is dense and conical. The needles cluster at branch tips. Attractive gray-black bark.

128. *Pinus strobus*, white pine

Height 50–80 ft., Zones 3–7

A beautiful native pine, pyramidal in youth, fast growing—with interesting structure—when older. Soft needles. It does not tolerate salt, so avoid planting it near a sidewalk or roadway that is salted during bad winter weather.

129. *Pinus sylvestris*, Scotch pine

Height 30–60 ft., Zones 3–7

With a little imaginative selective pruning from you, this can become quite an artistic plant. If you wait long enough, this will happen naturally, especially in an open, windswept environment.

130. *Pinus sylvestris* 'Watereri', Waterer Scotch pine

Height 25 ft., Zones 2–7

A cold-hardy, slow-growing cultivar with steel-blue needles. It does very well in the U.S. Midwest.

131. *Pinus thunbergii*, Japanese black pine

Height 20–80 ft., Zones 5–8

This pine is adaptable to either a wet or a dry climate.

132. *Pseudotsuga menziesii*, Douglas fir

Height 40–80 ft., Zones 4–6

This pyramidal evergreen has soft needles whose color varies from green to bluish. Use as a specimen or in a grouping. Tolerates light shade.

133. *Pseudotsuga menziesii* 'Glauca', blue Douglas fir

Height 40–80 ft., Zone 4

Bluer than other Douglas firs and widely adaptable to many landscape conditions.

134. *Thuja occidentalis*, American arborvitae

Height 40–60 ft., Zones 3–7

With a narrow, pyramidal structure, several of these trees will make a nice hedge.

135. *Thuja occidentalis* 'Nigra', dark green arborvitae

Height 20–30 ft., Zones 3–7

A pyramidal form with good, dark green foliage, this tree is natural in appearance, so it doesn't suffer from the stamped-out look of many arborvitae cultivars.

136. *Tsuga canadensis*, Canadian hemlock

Height 40–70 ft., Zones 3–7

Attractive glossy, dark foliage. This tree tolerates shade well and grows well in moist, well-drained, acid soil. Excellent for screening, in a grouping, or as an accent plant.

(Left) *Thuja occidentalis* 'Nigra'
(Right) *Tsuga canadensis*

LOW-GROWING EVERGREENS: 6 INCHES TO 6 FEET

As a group, low-growing evergreens are very versatile. Some are excellent hedge plants and tolerate pruning. Others are best used in natural plantings and look great in a screen planting. Some make for interesting specimen plants. And some species in this group perform great in dry, rocky conditions.

137. *Chamaecyparis obtusa* 'Nana', dwarf Hinoki falsecypress
Height 3 ft., Zones 5–8
This dwarf cultivar makes a specimen plant useful in a rock garden or a rock outcropping. It has dark green leaves and brown cones that are small, short, and orange tinged.

138. *Juniperus chinensis* 'Kallay Compacta', 'Kallay' juniper
Height 2 ft., Zones 4–9
This groundcover with blue-green foliage likes sun and good drainage.

139. *Juniperus chinensis* 'Sargentii', Sargent juniper
Height 18 in., Zones 4–9
Like *J. chinensis* 'Kallay Compacta', this blue-green groundcover likes sun and good drainage.

140. *Juniperus horizontalis* 'Hughes', 'Hughes' juniper
Height 2 ft., Zones 4–9
This low-growing juniper groundcover holds its blue-green in winter, with a tinge of plum color.

141. *Juniperus horizontalis* 'Wiltonii', blue rug juniper
Height 6 in., Zones 4–9
With silver-blue foliage, this juniper prefers sun and well-drained soil. Use as a rock garden plant cascading over a retaining wall.

142. *Juniperus procumbens*, Japanese juniper
Height 30 in., Zones 4–8
Use this low-spreading, full-sun evergreen as a groundcover in a rock garden or on a terrace.

143. *Juniperus procumbens* 'Nana', dwarf Japanese juniper
Height 2 ft., Zones 4–8
This low, blue-gray groundcover makes a very good rock garden plant. This cultivar is much more dense than the species, with a finer texture. Use on a hillside in full sun. It's also a great bonsai plant.

144. *Picea abies* 'Nidiformis', bird's nest spruce

Height 3–6 ft., Zones 3–7

A small yet broad and spreading cultivar. It usually has a depression in the center, giving the plant its name.

145. *Pinus mugo* var. *pumilio*, dwarf Mugo pine

Height 5 ft., Zones 4–5

This dwarf form is low growing and can be further reduced in height by annual pruning of the new growth (candles) in June. It has a round, mounded habit.

146. *Pinus mugo* var. *pumilio* 'Abruzzi-Maiella', dwarf Mugo pine

Height 3–6 ft., Zones 3–7 (8)

This dense, compact, dwarf cultivar is particularly drought tolerant.

147. *Taxus* x *media* 'Densiformis', Newport yew

Height 3 ft., Zones 4–7

Featuring bright green needles, this grows wider than it does tall. It does not like extreme heat; tolerates shade.

148. *Taxus* x *media* 'Taunton', 'Taunton' Yew

Height 3 ft., Zones 4–7

Tolerant of both heat and cold, as well as shade and pruning.

149. *Thuja occidentalis* 'Danica', 'Danica' arborvitae

Height 18 in., Zones 3–7

Dense, with glossy, emerald green foliage, this dwarf form is excellent as a low hedge.

Thuja occidentalis 'Danica'

150. *Thuja occidentalis* 'Holmstrup', 'Holmstrup' arborvitae

Height 6 ft., Zones 3–7

Compact and slow-growing, this is a narrow, pyramidal evergreen when used as a tall hedge. It tolerates pruning to keep it as a low hedge.

LARGE DECIDUOUS SHRUBS: 6 TO 15 FEET

There is tremendous variety among large deciduous shrubs. Usage varies from ornamental specimens to screen and hedge plants.

151. *Acer ginnala* 'Bailey's Compact', Bailey Amur maple

Height 6 ft., Zones 3–8

This smaller, compact form of *A. ginnala* has a finer branching structure than the species.

152. *Aesculus parviflora*, bottlebrush buckeye

Height 8–15 ft., Zones 4–8

Wide-spreading, multiple-stem shrub. The 8 to 10 in. flower panicles put on a spectacular display in June and July.

Aesculus parviflora

153. *Aronia arbutifolia* 'Brilliantisima', brilliant red chokeberry

Height 6 ft., Zones 4–9

Upright, colonizing shrub. The white flowers in May are followed by attractive red fruit that will persist through the winter months. The foliage has excellent scarlet fall color.

Aronia arbutifolia
'Brilliantisima'

154. *Aronia melanocarpa*, black chokeberry

Height 6 ft., Zones 4–9

Similar to red chokeberry, A. *arbutifolia*, but with black fruit and purplish red fall color. Tolerant of moist areas.

155. *Buddleia davidii*, butterfly bush

Height 6 ft., Zones 4–5

Plant this to attract butterflies, as they love the flowers. This shrub can be found with every flower color. It doesn't fill space year-round. In Zone 5 it should be pruned to the ground in the fall and mulched, or pruned back in the spring. In Zone 4 the plant will die back to the ground on its own.

156. *Calycanthus floridus*, Carolina allspice, common sweetshrub

Height 6 ft., Zones 4–9

This shrub has lustrous, dark green leaves and June flowers with some fragrance. The fruit is a 2 in., reddish brown capsule in an interesting urn shape.

157. *Cephalanthus occidentalis*, button bush

Height 8 ft., Zones 5–11

This shrub has attractive late-leafing foliage and creamy white flowers, which are followed by fruit that persists through the winter. It is best in a moist area.

158. *Chaenomeles speciosa*, common flowering quince

Height 6–10 ft., Zones 4–8 (9)

Excellent flowering shrub with many different colors, usually a shade or orange or red, depending on cultivar.

159. *Clethra alnifolia*, summersweet clethra

Height 6 ft., Zones 4–9

Fragrant white flowers from July into August. Handsome foliage. Numerous cultivars are available.

160. *Cornus amomum*, silky dogwood
Height 6–10 ft., Zones 4–8
This shrub border plant displays yellowish white flowers in May. Birds enjoy the bluish berries in August.

161. *Cornus racemosa*, gray dogwood
Height 12 ft., Zones 3–8
White flowers bloom in May to June, followed by bluish white berries. This colonizing shrub tolerates some shade and does best in a moist, well-drained location.

162. *Cornus sericea*, redosier dogwood
Height 8 ft., Zones 2–7
Use in a shrub border. The red stems give winter interest to the garden. Tolerant of moisture.

163. *Cornus sericea* 'Flaviramea', yellow twig dogwood
Height 6–8 ft., Zones 2–7
Multistemmed shrub whose yellow stems provide winter interest.

164. *Corylus americana*, American filbert
Height 12 ft., Zones 4–9
This multiple-stem shrub is wonderful for naturalizing in sun to light shade. It has interesting yellowish-brown flowers, nutlike fruit, and burnt-orange fall foliage.

Corylus americana

165. *Cotinus coggygria*, smoketree
Height 10–15 ft., Zones 4–8
Most interesting as a multiple-stem plant or when used in a shrub border, it has blue-green foliage and, from June to August, smoky pink flowering panicles.

166. *Cotoneaster divaricatus*, spreading cotoneaster
Height 6 ft., Zones 4–7
Lustrous small, green leaves and handsome red fruit. The slightly pendulous branching habit creates an attractive appearance. The excellent texture associates well with other plants.

167. *Cotoneaster lucidus*, Peking cotoneaster
Height 6–10 ft., Zones 4–7
This ideal hedge plant has pinkish white flowers in May.

168. *Cotoneaster multiflorus*, many-flowered cotoneaster

Height 8–12 ft., Zones 4–7

Attractive gray-green foliage, abundant white flowers in May, red berries.

169. *Deutzia scabra*, fuzzy deutzia

Height 6–10 ft., Zones 5–7

Pubescent leaves give this oval, round-topped shrub its common name. Attractive white flower panicles, sometimes tinged pink, bloom in June. The stems are brown and peeling, giving the shrub a somewhat straggly appearance.

170. *Enkianthus campanulatus*, redvein enkianthus

Height 6–8 ft., Zones 5–7

This narrow, upright shrub has bright green to dull blue-green leaves with some hairs. Beautiful, dainty, creamy yellow to light orange pendulous flowers bloom in May to June. The leaves turn yellow, orange, and red in fall.

171. *Euonymus alatus*, winged euonymus

Height 12 ft., Zones 4–8

Strong, attractive appearance. Grown for bark interest; shape—wider than tall; and fall color.

172. *Euonymus alatus* 'Compactus', dwarf burning bush

Height 6–10 ft., Zones 4–7

Slow-growing and with a dense structure, this is a rounded form that seldom requires pruning. Excellent scarlet fall color.

173. *Forsythia intermedia*, border forsythia

Height 8–10 ft., Zones 4–9

This border shrub blooms in March to April with yellow flowers. It's an excellent plant for forcing blooms indoors.

174. *Forsythia suspensa*, weeping forsythia

Height 10 ft., Zones 5–8

Upright, arching habit. There are yellow flowers in early spring and yellow fall color. Plant in full sun for optimal blooming.

175. *Fothergilla major*, large fothergilla

Height 10 ft., Zones 4–8

Dark green to blue-green leaves. White, flowering, fragrant, bottlebrush-like spikes bloom in April to May. The fall color ranges from yellow to orange to scarlet.

176. *Hamamelis mollis*, Chinese witch hazel

Height 10–15 ft., Zones 5–8

Fragrant yellow flowers with red centers bloom in February to March. The foliage has yellow to yellow-orange fall color, with black berries.

177. *Hamamelis virginiana*, common witch hazel

Height 15 ft., Zones 3–9

This large shrub or small tree has fragrant, yellow flowers in October. Shade tolerant.

178. *Hydrangea paniculata* 'Chantilly Lace', 'Chantilly Lace' hydrangea

Height 8 ft., Zones 3–8

The large, white blooms—which turn deep pink—are cone-shaped and lacy. Sturdy stems hold the clusters upright. This variety is very hardy in summer heat and does well in either sun or shade.

179. *Hydrangea paniculata* 'Compacta', compact PeeGee hydrangea

Height 6 ft., Zones 3–8

Similar to PeeGee hydrangea, *H. paniculata* 'Grandiflora', in blooming period and fall color, this is a compact form with smaller leaves and blooms.

180. *Hydrangea paniculata* 'Grandiflora', PeeGee hydrangea

Height 8 ft., Zones 3–8

Attractive and showy double, white flowers bloom from July to September. This plant also has dark green leaves and an upright habit.

181. *Hydrangea paniculata* 'Passionate', passionate hydrangea

Height 8 ft., Zones 3–8

Creamy white blooms are on display from July into fall. This hydrangea prefers moist, well-drained soil and partial shade.

182. *Hydrangea paniculata* 'Tardiva', 'Tardiva' hydrangea

Height 8 ft., Zones 3–8

This shrub grows up to 10 ft. wide. With a later blooming period than PeeGee hydrangea (*H. paniculata* 'Grandiflora'), the lacy, 6 in., white, blooms of 'Tardiva' turn pink in late summer. Sturdy stems keep the flowers upright.

183. *Ilex decidua*, possumhaw

Height 7–15 ft., Zones 5–9

Large shrub with a lot of branching horizontally. The glossy, dark green foliage turns yellow in fall. White flowers. Orange to scarlet fruit ripens in September and persists into spring. The beautiful gray bark also stands out in winter. This plant needs a lot of space; it has the potential to grow very large.

184. *Ilex verticillata*, winterberry holly
Height 10 ft., Zones 3–9
This deciduous holly, without rival in the winter landscape, is grown for its colorful red berries. Separate female and male plants are needed to produce the berries. Can handle moisture.

Ilex verticillata

185. *Kerria japonica*, Kerry bush
Height 6 ft., Zones 5–9
Greenish stems provide winter interest. Bright yellow flowers bloom in April. This shrub requires partial shade, not direct sun.

186. *Kolkwitzia amabilis*, beauty bush
Height 10 ft., Zones 4–8
This has a beautiful arching habit and, in June, clusters of pink flowers. The foliage turns red in fall. The shrub prefers full sun but will tolerate partial shade.

187. *Laburnum* x *watereri*, goldenchain tree
Height 12 ft., Zones 5–7
With interesting olive green bark on young trees and fragrant, yellow flowers in May, this shrub makes for an attractive display in a shrub border.

188. *Lindera benzoin*, spicebush\
Height 6–12 ft., Zones 4–9
This rounded shrub has light green foliage that turns yellow in the fall. Attractive yellow flowers in April. A good plant to use in a shrub border or to naturalize an area, it grows in either sun or shade and is excellent for moist areas.

189. *Lonicera fragrantissima*, winter honeysuckle
Height 6–10 ft., Zones 4–8
In March to April this wide-spreading, rounded shrub bears extremely fragrant lemon-scented flowers that are creamy white tinged with pink.

190. *Magnolia liliflora*, lily magnolia
Height 8–10 ft., Zones 5–8
The beautiful 3 to 4 in. wide flower, purple outside and white inside, blooms in May.

191. *Malus halliana* 'Adirondack', Adirondack crabapple

Height 10 ft., Zones 4–7

Red flower buds open white with a red tinge. The fruit is red to orange-red. Columnar habit.

192. *Malus sargentii*, Sargent flowering crabapple

Height 10–12 ft., Zones 4–7

This excellent small tree has dark green foliage; fragrant, single, red flowers; and bright red to deep purple fruit. The horizontal growth is picturesque, reaching 18 ft. wide, well exceeding the height.

193. *Myrica pensylvanica*, northern bayberry

Height 6–12 ft., Zones 3–6

Semi-evergreen to evergreen, colonizing shrub. Fragrant foliage and fragrant gray-white berries. This shrub likes full sun to partial shade and tolerates moisture. Separate male and female plants are necessary for fruiting.

194. *Photinia villosa*, Oriental Photina

Height 10–15 ft., Zones 4–7

Grow as a shrub or small, trained tree in full sun or light shade. Somewhat vase-shaped in habit. The attractive foliage changes to yellowish, red-bronze, and red in fall. The white flowers of May and June are followed by bright red fruit in October.

195. *Physocarpus opulifolius*, common ninebark

Height 5–10 ft., Zones 2–7

Easily transplanted, this shrub adapts to less-than-perfect situations and likes full sun or partial shade. However, its straggly habit and limited ornamental interest make it difficult to use in small home landscapes.

196. *Pyracantha coccinea*, scarlet firethorn

Height 6–12 ft., Zones 6–9

Large shrub that needs pruning to keep it manageable. Thorny branches with white flowers and orange-red fruit. Spectacular winter color.

197. *Rhododendron* 'Schlippenbachii', royal azalea

Height 6 ft., Zones 4–6

This is the earliest rhododendron to bloom, with fragrant, rose-pink flowers in May. The dark green foliage turns to crimson-orange in fall. Top honors for this azalea.

198. *Rhus aromatica*, fragrant sumac
Height 2–6 ft., Zones 3–9
With an irregular spreading habit due to suckers, this can be used for screening or as a windbreak. Small yellow flowers bloom in March to April, followed by hairy, red fruit. Orange to red to purple fall leaf color.

199. *Sambucus canadensis*, American elder
Height 5–12 ft., Zones (3) 4–9
This large shrub is known for its clusters of bluish black berries that are used in jam, jelly, wine, and pie. Small, profuse creamy-white flowers June to July. Use in areas you want to naturalize.

200. *Sorbaria sorbifolia*, Ural falsespirea
Height 5–10 ft., Zones 2–7
Ornamental, multistemmed shrub with attractive fernlike leaves that leaf out early in the spring. It is fast growing and spreads by suckers. Attractive blooms.

201. *Stewartia ovata*, mountain stewartia
Height 10–15 ft., Zones 5–8
A large shrub or small tree with white flowers, stewartia should be used as a specimen plant and put where it can be seen. Its fall color and bark are among the best.

202. *Syringa meyeri*, dwarf Korean lilac
Height 6 ft., Zones 3–7
This lilac blooms profusely with fragrant, violet-purple flowers in May, even when small. It has an orderly structure.

203. *Syringa patula* 'Miss Kim',
Miss Kim Korean lilac
Height 6 ft., Zones 3–7
The leaves are slightly larger than those of *S. meyeri*. It has violet-blue flowers and a uniform habit.

Syringa patula 'Miss Kim'

204. *Viburnum burkwoodii*, Burkwood viburnum
Height 6 ft., Zones 5–8
The flowers are pink in bud, opening to fragrant white in May. Use where flower fragrance can be enjoyed indoors. Semi-evergreen to evergreen. Judicious pruning is sometimes necessary.

Viburnum carlesii

205. *Viburnum carlesii*, **Koreanspice viburnum**
Height 6 ft., Zones 4–7
These flowers are also pink in bud, opening to fragrant white in May. Excellent fall foliage color in a sunny location.

206. *Viburnum cassinoides*, **Witherod viburnum**
Height 6 ft., Zones 5–9
Attractive dense and shapely shrub. White flowers bloom in June to July. The fruit is the highlight of this shrub, as it goes through a process of turning green to pink, then red to blue, and sometimes showing all colors at once. The dark green foliage changes to orange, red, and purple in the fall. A naturalizing gem.

207. *Viburnum dentatum*, **arrowwood viburnum**
Height 8 ft., Zones 2–8
This is a multiple-stemmed shrub that colonizes, making it an excellent screening shrub for sun to partial shade. Creamy white flowers are followed by blue berries that birds love to eat. The lustrous, dark green leaves turn reddish purple in the fall.

Viburnum dentatum

208. *Viburnum dentatum* Blue Muffin, **Blue Muffin viburnum**
Height 7 ft., Zones 2–8
This compact variety produces lacy, white flowers in spring, followed by shiny clusters of blue berries. Adaptable to sun and shade.

209. *Viburnum dentatum* Chicago Lustre, **Chicago Lustre arrowwood viburnum**
Height 10 ft., Zones 2–8
This is an upright shrub with glossy, dark green leaves that turn yellow to reddish purple in fall; Creamy white flower clusters in June; and bluish black berries in fall and winter.

210. *Viburnum dilatatum*, linden viburnum

Height 10 ft., Zones 4–7

White flowers bloom in May to early June, followed by red fruit in the fall, persisting into winter. A special, all-season beauty with positive plant characteristics.

211. *Viburnum lantana* 'Mohican', 'Mohican' viburnum

Height 7 ft., Zones 3–8

This dense, compact viburnum has dark green leaves that turn purplish red in fall. Creamy white flowers in spring are followed by orange-red to black berries. The shrub is disease resistant and prefers full sun but tolerates partial shade.

212. *Viburnum plicatum* var. *tomentosa*, doublefile viburnum

Height 10 ft., Zones 5–7

The attractive pure-white flowers in May grab your attention, as does the interesting horizontal, layered branching structure. Bright red fruit in the fall. Hardiness is a question; plant in a protected area. Numerous cultivars are available.

213. *Viburnum prunifolium*, blackhaw viburnum

Height 12 ft., Zones 3–9

Grow as a multiple-stemmed shrub or small tree. It has interesting horizontal branching. Creamy white flowers in May are followed by pinkish rose to bluish black fruit. Purple to red fall foliage.

214. *Viburnum sargentii*, Sargent viburnum

Height 12 ft., Zones 3–7

Creamy white flower clusters 3 to 6 in. in diameter bloom in late May. Beautiful rose-red fruit.

215. *Viburnum trilobum*, American cranberry bush viburnum

Height 8–12 ft., Zones 2–7

Known for its edible, scarlet berries, this shrub displays flat, creamy white flower clusters in May and red foliage in fall.

216. *Viburnum trilobum* 'Wentworth', 'Wentworth' viburnum

Height 12 ft., Zones 2–7

The attractive white flowers of late May are followed by bright red fruit from September into February. This makes a nice screening plant but requires good drainage.

SMALL TO MEDIUM DECIDUOUS SHRUBS: 2 TO 5 FEET

Small- to medium-sized deciduous shrubs range in use from hedge shrubs to single specimen plants. Since they're smaller than most trees and shrubs, they are usually planted closer to the house, around the patio or deck, and at the front entrance. For this same reason, they are not very effective in perimeter screen plantings.

217. *Berberis koreana*, Korean barberry
Height 4–6 ft., Zones 3–7
This multistemmed, oval shrub will form a colony by sucker growth. Medium to dark green leaves. There are one to five spines on each stem. The showy yellow flowers in May are eventually followed by bright red fruit in fall through winter.

218. *Berberis* x *mentorensis*, mentor barberry
Height 5–7 ft., Zones 5–8
Use this upright, bushy, rounded shrub as a small hedge or border plant. There are dark green leaves, turning yellow-orange to red in the fall, and three spines per stem. Attractive yellow flowers bloom in April to May.

219. *Berberis thunbergi* 'Kobold', Kobold barberry
Height 2 ft., Zones 4–8
This barberry has a compact, low mounding habit and attractive lustrous foliage. Its red berries are a landscape asset.

220. *Ceanothus americanus*, New Jersey tea
Height 3–4 ft., Zones 4–8
This small, compact shrub has an upright branching structure and a rounded habit. Showy 1 to 2 in., white flower panicles bloom in June and July. It tolerates dryness and does fine in either full sun or shade.

221. *Chaenomeles speciosa* 'Texas Scarlet', 'Texas Scarlet' quince
Height 3 ft., Zones 4–8
This is the best red-flowering quince. Compact, spreading growth.

222. *Clethra alnifolia* 'Hummingbird', 'Hummingbird' clethra
Height 3 ft., Zones 4–9
One of the best compact deciduous shrubs, it has 6 in. long white flowers in June and golden yellow fall color.

223. *Clethra alnifolia* 'Ruby Spice', 'Ruby Spice' clethra
Height 3 ft., Zones 4–9
Pink flowering in July or August.

224. *Cornus sericea* 'Kelseyi', Kelsey dwarf dogwood

Height 3 ft., Zones 2–7

Plant this in the shrub border. Its compact habit also makes it ideal for use in masses. There are small, white, flower clusters, and its red stems provide winter garden interest.

225. *Cotoneaster apiculatus*, cranberry cotoneaster

Height 3 ft., Zones 4–6

This low-spreading groundcover cascades over walls. It features attractive small leaves, pink flowers in May, red berries, and excellent fall color.

226. *Cotoneaster horizontalis*, rockspray cotoneaster

Height 2 ft., Zones 5–7

Attractive small, reddish purple leaves, pink flowers in May and June, and red berries.

227. *Deutzia gracilis*, slender deutzia

Height 2–4 ft., Zones 4–8

A small, graceful, mounded shrub that is covered in perfect white flowers in May. It has bright to deep green leaves but no effective fall color.

228. *Dirca palustris*, leatherwood

Height 3–6 ft., Zones 4–9

This plant needs to grow in shade and enjoys moist soil. Pale yellow flowers bloom in March to April.

229. *Forsythia viridissima* 'Bronxensis', Bronx forsythia

Height 2 ft., Zones 5–8

Yellow flowers bloom in spring if the winter was mild. Even without flowers, the dense growth helps make it one of our few good dwarf plants.

230. *Fothergilla gardenii*, dwarf fothergilla

Height 3 ft., Zones 4–8

Leatherlike, dark green leaves, then yellow-orange to scarlet fall color. Fragrant, white flowers bloom in April to early May. This shrub likes moist soil and partial shade and is very attractive set among other plants. Numerous good cultivars are available.

231. *Genista tinctoria*, common woadwaxen

Height 2–3 ft., Zones 4–7

This small, spiky shrub with an upright, vertical-branching habit adds color to the garden. The bright green leaf color does not change in fall, but the yellow flowers peak in June and continue through September. This is a good plant for poor, dry soil conditions.

232. *Hydrangea arborescens* 'Annabelle', 'Annabelle' hydrangea

Height 4 ft., Zones 4–9

The large June flowers droop from relatively weak branches, so avoid giving this shrub a prominent location in the garden.

233. *Hydrangea quercifolia*, oakleaf hydrangea

Height 4–6 ft., Zones 5–9

The large, oaklike leaves make excellent foliage, especially with the plant's upright branching. Large, fragrant, white flowers in June change to purplish pink. This hydrangea likes shade and moisture.

234. *Hypericum prolificum*, St. John's wort

Height 1–4 ft., Zones 4–8

This small, dense shrub is best used in the shrub border fronting larger shrubs or evergreens. Bright yellow, ¾ to 1 in. flowers bloom in June through August.

235. *Ilex verticillata* 'Red Sprite', 'Red Sprite' winterberry holly

Height 3–5 ft., Zones 3–9

Excellent female winterberry holly. Production of the persistent bright red berries requires a male pollinator. The dark green leaves do not change color in fall.

236. *Kerria japonica* 'Golden Guinea', 'Golden Guinea' kerria

Height 4–5 ft., Zones 4–9

This shrub has a compact habit with bright green leaves and stems. Round, golden-yellow flowers. It does not tolerate afternoon sun.

237. *Physocarpus opulifolius* 'Nanus', dwarf ninebark

Height 3 ft., Zones 2–7

The small, dark green leaves change into excellent fall color. Best of all the ninebarks, use this variety as a hedge.

238. *Potentilla fruticosa* 'Gold Drop', 'Gold Drop' potentilla

Height 3 ft., Zones 2–6

A compact variety with deep yellow flowers that bloom all summer long.

239. *Rhododendron mucronulatum*, Korean rhododendron

Height 4–8 ft., Zones 4–7

The plant leafs out in early April, and the rose-purple flowers bloom in early to mid-May. Trouble free and very hardy.

240. *Rhodotypos scandens*, black jetbead

Height 4–6 ft., Zones 4–8

Attractive shiny leaves, white flowers in June, and shiny, beadlike, black fruit. This trouble-free shrub tolerates either sun or shade.

241. *Rhus aromatica* 'Gro-Low', grow-low sumac

Height 2 ft., Zones 3–9

This groundcover with small, glossy leaves thrives in sunny areas. It displays excellent orange-red fall color and red fruit.

242. *Ribes alpinum* 'Aureum', golden currant

Height 3–6 ft., Zones 2–7

Upright, erect habit. The attractive 2 in. long, bright golden yellow flowers are fragrant. The berries attract birds. This shrub has good red fall color.

243. *Ribes alpinum* 'Green Mound', 'Green Mound' alpine currant

Height 4 ft., Zones 2–7

Excellent as a hedge, this currant has dark green leaves and is shade tolerant.

244. *Ribes alpinum* 'Pumila', dwarf alpine currant

Height 2 ft., Zones 2–7

Interesting branching habit with dark green leaves. Use this shade-tolerant plant as a low hedge.

245. *Spiraea* x *bumalda* 'Anthony Waterer', 'Anthony Waterer' spirea

Height 3 ft., Zones 3–8

Allow this low, small-leaved shrub to grow together with others of its kind. Pinkish red flowers bloom in June to July. Wine red fall color. Prune it after flowering, and it will bloom again in the fall, but do not prune into a ball.

246. *Spiraea* x *bumalda* 'Coccinea', dwarf red spirea

Height 2–3 ft., Zones 3–8

This dense shrub with a rounded habit has more flowers and a more uniform structure than 'Anthony Waterer'. Flowers are bright carmine red.

247. *Spiraea* x *bumalda* 'Crispa', crisp-leaf spirea

Height 2–3 ft., Zones 3–8

Twisted, deeply serrated leaves. The rose-pink flowers bloom in 3 in. clusters in June to July. This variety is even more compact than 'Anthony Waterer'.

248. *Spiraea* x *bumala* 'Froebelii', Froebel spirea

Height 4 ft., Zones 3–8

Rounded habit. Flat, rose-pink flower clusters bloom in May to June. The new growth is purplish green.

249. *Spiraea nipponica*, snowmound spirea

Height 3–5 ft., Zones 4–7

Excellent growth. This spirea has dark blue-green leaves and white flowers blooming in late May to June.

250. *Spiraea thunbergii*, Japanese spirea

Height 3–5 ft., Zones 4–8

The light green foliage contrasts nicely with most shrubs, which have darker green leaves. Bronze leaf color in the fall. White flowers bloom in March to April. Prune after flowering.

251. *Stephanandra incisa* 'Crispa', cutleaf stephanandra

Height 2 ft., Zones 4–7

This graceful shrub, with dense, fine-textured foliage and yellowish white flowers in May to June, makes a good groundcover for slopes. The bright green leaves turn reddish orange in the fall.

BROADLEAF EVERGREENS: 1 FOOT AND LARGER

The broadleaf evergreens add much interest to the garden. These plants are green year-round and have flat leaves similar to those of a deciduous plant. Certain varieties make great hedge plants. Others make for compelling specimen or grouping plants.

252. *Berberis julianae*, wintergreen barberry

Height 6 ft., Zones 5–8

Attractive dense foliage. Use this in a shrub border.

253. *Buxus microphylla koreana* 'Wintergreen', 'Wintergreen' boxwood
Height 3–4 ft., Zones 4–8
Small, light green, evergreen leaves. This cultivar tolerates colder climates. Excellent as a low evergreen hedge, it can be kept 18–24 in. high.

254. *Euonymus fortunei* 'Sarcoxie', 'Sarcoxie' euonymus
Height 4 ft., Zones 4–8
An upright, small, shiny-leafed evergreen, this bushy shrub is very manageable and tolerates pruning. It does better in shade than sun.

255. *Ilex crenata*, Japanese holly
Height 5–10 ft., Zones 5–6
Dark green with elliptical-shaped leaves, this evergreen is dense and multistemmed. The female plant produces a black, berrylike fruit in September to October. An excellent addition to the garden for texture, use it in a mass or a hedge.

256. *Ilex glabra*, inkberry
Height 6 ft., Zones 4–9
Evergreen, lustrous, dark green leaves and black berries. It likes moist, acidic soil and is best in sun. It will tolerate pruning, so you can use it as a tall hedge or an accent plant.

257. *Ilex pedunculosa*, longstalk holly
Height 15 ft., Zone 5
This large shrub or small tree is the hardiest of the evergreen, red-fruiting hollies. It's a very attractive plant with lustrous, dark green leaves. Not heat tolerant in warmer zones.

258. *Itea virginica*, Virginia sweetspice
Height 3–8 ft., Zones 5–9
This semi-evergreen to evergreen shrub enjoys moist soil. White flowers bloom in May to June. The attractive leaves change to yellow, orange, reddish purple, scarlet, and crimson in the fall.

259. *Kalmia latifolia*, mountain laurel
Height 8 ft., Zones 4–9
This large evergreen shrub is dense and symmetrical as a juvenile, but open and straggly, with picturesque branching, when older. The light green to bronze foliage changes to dark green with age. The highlight of this plant is the flowers, which bloom from May to June. They are white to rose-pink to deep rose. The shrub requires acidic, moist, well-drained soil. Sun is best for flower production, but the plant does well in either full sun or deep shade. Excellent for naturalizing.

260. *Lavandula angustifolia*, common lavender, English lavender

Height 1–2 ft., Zones 5–8

Gray to bluish green, semievergreen leaves. The abundant, attractive lavender-purple flower spikes bloom in June, July, or August and are very fragrant. This plant is the source of lavender oil. Use in a herb garden, a small shrub border, or a low hedge.

261. *Leucothoe fontanesiana*, drooping leucothoe

Height 3–6 ft., Zones 5–8

The leathery, dark green, evergreen leaves turn purple-bronze in winter. White, urn-shaped flowers are sometimes hidden under the leaves. The graceful arching habit with long leaves makes this an attractive plant.

262. *Mahonia aquifolium*, Oregon grape holly

Height 6 ft., Zones 4–7

The lustrous, hollylike evergreen foliage turns purplish green in the fall. Upright habit. The yellow flowers in April are followed by attractive blue berries late in the summer and into fall. Tolerates shade. Use in a protected area.

263. *Pieris japonica*, Japanese pieris

Height 6 ft., Zones 4–7

This evergreen plant requires a protected area, not the open, windswept ones most broadleaf evergreens withstand. It also requires moist, acidic, well-drained soil. The flowers are fragrant, pendulous, white panicles. This shrub does well in sun or partial shade, as in a shrub border.

264. *Rhododendron* 'Aglo', 'Aglo' rhododendron

Height 5 ft., Zones 4–5

The light pink flowers bloom in April to May.

265. *Rhododendron carolinianum*, Carolina rhododendron

Height 3–6 ft., Zones (4) 5–8

This is a low-growing, rounded, broadleaf evergreen shrub with dark green leaves. The flowers vary in color from pure white to pale rose. Plant in a slightly shaded area with well-drained soil and out of strong winter winds.

266. *Rhododendron catawbiense*, Catawba rhododendron

Height 6–10 ft., Zones 4–8

A handsome broadleaf evergreen with a spread of 5–8 ft. Its flowers are lilac-purple to purple-rose and bloom in mid-to-late May. The cultivar 'Nova Zembla' is quite hardy.

267. *Rhododendron* Gable Hybrids, Gable hybrid azaleas

Height 4 ft., Zone 5

There are many good choices in this evergreen hybrid series, including 'Karen', with lavender-pink flowers in April to May. The flower color in the series ranges from white to pink to purple to red to orange.

268. *Rhododendron* 'Olga Mezitt', Olga rhododendron

Height 6 ft., Zones 4–6

This reliable, upright, spreading evergreen shrub has compact, peach-pink flowers in May. The foliage turns light red in fall.

269. *Rhododendron* 'P.J.M.', P.J.M. rhododendron

Height 5 ft., Zone 4

Easy to grow, with purple-pink flowers.

Rhododendron 'P.J.M.'

VINES AND GROUNDCOVERS

Groundcovers are great for unifying a garden. They can densely fill in an area at ground level. Many varieties are also evergreen, providing year-round color. Vines offer interest on vertical structures and are great for softening such hard materials as fences, walls, and trellises.

270. *Ampelopsis brevipedunculata*, porcelain ampelopsis

Height 10–25 ft., Zones 4–8

Use this fast-growing vine to cover unsightly objects. Dark green, usually three-lobed leaves. The very attractive fruit ranges from yellow to lilac to amethyst in September to October.

271. *Arctostaphylos uva-ursi*, bearberry

Height 6–12 in., Zones 2–6

This low, glossy, evergreen groundcover can cover a large area. The leaves turn bronze to red in the winter. Delicate, white to pinkish flowers in April to May are followed by lustrous, bright red fruit in July and August and into fall.

272. *Aristolochia macrophylla*, Dutchman's pipe

Height 20–30 ft., Zones 4–8

A vigorous vine historically used to screen and cover front porches, it has large, attractive leaves that form a solid screen. The yellow-green flowers, which give the plant its name, are borne in May or June. Very adaptable to most soils as long as the ground is moist and well-drained.

273. *Asarum europaeum*, European ginger

Height 6–8 in., Zones 4–7

This is a beautiful evergreen groundcover for a moist, shaded site. Glossy, heart-shaped leaves.

Asarum europaeum

274. *Campsis radicans*, trumpet vine

Height 30–40 ft., Zones 4–9

This vigorous vine needs ample room to grow. Its scarlet, trumpet-shaped flowers are approximately 3 in. long. Grow on a large trellis or fence.

(Left) *Campsis radicans*

(Right and bottom)
Clematis jackmanii

275. *Celastrus scandens*, American bittersweet

Height 20 ft., Zones 3–8

A vigorous, twining vine that can form a shrublike appearance, it will consume any fence. Deciduous, lustrous, dark green leaves. Use carefully to hide rock piles, old trees, fences, or other rough, unsightly areas. Fast-growing, it will strangle, girdle, and eventually kill trees and shrubs.

276. *Clematis jackmanii*, Jackman clematis

Height 10 ft., Zones 4–8

Large, violet-purple flowers bloom from June till frost. There are numerous cultivars and species of this good vine. Mulch the base to keep the roots cool. Unlike many other clematises, this is not invasive.

277. *Clematis tangutica*, golden clematis

Height 10 ft., Zones 5–7

This climbing vine bears 3 to 4 in., golden yellow, lantern-shaped flowers in June and July.

278. *Convallaria majalis*, lily of the valley

Height 8–12 in., Zones 2–7

This is a shade-tolerant groundcover, but it can also be grown in the sun. Fragrant white, bell-shaped flowers in late spring.

279. *Cornus canadensis*, bunchberry

Height 3–9 in., Zones 2–6

This slow-spreading groundcover performs best in cold climates. The dark green leaves appear to be whorled. The plant prefers full or partial shade and organic, rich, acidic soil. Site it under acid-loving evergreens. There's a showy scarlet-colored, berrylike drupe in August, persisting into fall. The leaves turn red in fall.

280. *Cotoneaster dammeri*, bearberry cotoneaster

Height 1–1½ ft., Zones 5–7

Evergreen to semievergreen foliage with bright red fruit. Since it has a spreading habit, use this plant as a groundcover, such as on slopes.

281. *Daphne cneorum*, garland flower

Height 6–12 in., Zones 4–7

This broadleaf evergreen is 6–12 in. tall by 30 in. wide. Fragrant pink flowers bloom in April to May. Dark green foliage.

282. *Euonymus fortunei* 'Coloratus', purpleleaf wintercreeper

Height 12 in., Zones 4–8

This is an excellent evergreen groundcover or vine. The green leaves change to purple in fall. Aggressive and requiring annual pruning when set near shrubs or other plants, it'll climb and attach to whatever it touches. One of the best groundcovers.

283. *Euonymus fortunei* 'Vegetus', bigleaf wintercreeper

Height 4 ft., Zones 4–8

This evergreen groundcover or vine with attractive leaves will climb when grown against walls, arbors, trellises, and so on. Green to orange berries. It can become a shrublike evergreen.

284. *Hedera helix*, English ivy

Height 8 in., Zones 4–9

This shade-tolerant evergreen groundcover is often seen growing on walls of homes and university buildings. There are numerous good cultivars, 'Bulgaria' being one of the hardiest.

285. *Hedera helix* 'Thorndale', Thorndale English ivy

Height 6–8 in., Zones 4–9

Evergreen groundcover and vine with larger leaves than the species. Shade tolerant.

286. *Hydrangea anomala petiolaris*, climbing hydrangea

Height 20 ft., Zone 5

A vigorous vine, and one of the most attractive, it grows to 20 ft. and possibly greater. Attractive heart-shaped leaves; creamy white flowers in June; interesting, attractive bark in winter. Does well in full sun or partial shade.

287. *Iberis sempervirens*, candytuft

Height 6–12 in., Zones 4–8

Low-growing, spreading evergreen groundcover. It is early blooming, in April to May; the flowers last several weeks.

288. *Lonicera* x *heckrottii*, goldflame honeysuckle

Vine, Zones 4–9

The most handsome of the climbing honeysuckles. In April, the carmine flower buds open to a creamy yellow inside and gradually fade to pink on the outside. Very handsome.

Pachysandra terminalis

289. *Pachysandra terminalis*, Japanese spurge
Height 10 in., Zones 4–6
This evergreen groundcover with white flowers does best in shade.

290. *Parthenocissus quinquefolia*, Virginia creeper
Height 30–50 ft., Zones 4–9
A deciduous vine growing 6–10 ft. in one season. A bluish black berry ripens in September to October. Excellent fall color. Use on walls and trellises.

291. *Paxistima canbyi*, Canby paxistima
Height 12 in., Zones 3–7
This is a low-growing groundcover, 12 in. high by 3–4 ft. wide. The lustrous, dark green foliage of summer turns bronze in the winter. This plant prefers moist, well-drained soil in full sun or partial shade.

292. *Polygonum aubertii*, silver-vine fleece flower
Height 25–35 ft., Zones 4–7
Fast-growing, twining, deciduous vine. The leaves emerge a reddish color but turn a bright green. Fragrant white, greenish white, or slightly pink flower panicles bloom in July to August.

293. *Polygonum reynoutria*, low Japanese fleece flower
Height 2 ft., Zones 4–8
This wide-spreading, deciduous groundcover bears white flowers and reddish fruit.

294. *Sedum spurium* 'Dragon's Blood', 'Dragon's Blood' stonecrop
Height 3–6 in., Zones 3–8
A herbaceous groundcover that likes the sun. Rose-red flowers. It's excellent when used behind walls, between flagstone in retaining walls, and in rock gardens.

Sedum spurium
'Dragon's Blood'

295. *Sedum kamtschaticum*, stonecrop
Height 6–8 in., Zones 3–8
This groundcover has orangish yellow flowers. Flowers from July to August.

296. *Teucrium chamaedrys*, wall germander
Height 12 in., Zones 5–8
A low, mounded evergreen groundcover with dark green leaves, it can be used as a low hedge or a rock garden plant. Rose-purple flowers bloom from June to September.

297. *Thymus citriodorus*, lemon thyme
Height 8–12 in., Zones 4–7
This groundcover features a lemon fragrance and pale purple flowers. Use it in a rock garden or a rock grouping.

298. *Vinca minor*, periwinkle
Height 6–12 in., Zones 3–8
An evergreen groundcover with purple flowers.

299. *Vinca minor* 'Bowles', La Graves periwinkle
Height 6–12 in., Zones 3–8
Evergreen with dark blue flowers.

300. *Wisteria floribunda*, Japanese wisteria
Height 30 ft., Zones 4–9
Interesting compound leaves. Violet or violet-blue, 18 to 20 in. racemes flower in April to May. Vines will twine together clockwise. A plant's size is determined only by the structure on which it grows.

Conclusion

From the broad principles of good landscaping design to the details of smart plant choices, we've covered a lot of material. But have we covered every aspect of landscaping? Not even close.

The practice of landscaping and gardening is a lifelong endeavor. It is a practice that is consistent in plan, yet evolutionary in detail. By learning the fundamentals of landscaping and establishing a thoughtful design at the outset of your projects, you will avoid many pitfalls during the initial landscape development and as your landscape grows through the years. The work of landscaping your property requires patience, but the payoff is great. As reward for your dedication, you get the pride and pleasure of having cultivated a landscape you can enjoy every day, through the seasons, year after year.

Landscape gardening is meant to be enjoyable, therapeutic, satisfying, and most of all, fun. Good planning makes that possible. In fact, taking the time and care for good planning can deliver more pleasure from your landscape than you ever expected. As one long-term client shared with us, "I only planned on doing the basics when my house was built. But, after what turned out to be the first of many phases, I was so pleased that over the next few years I developed my entire property. I never imagined my property could become what it is now. I rarely spent time outside before, but now I have a place to go!"

As your knowledge about plants and garden design grows, you will better be able to distinguish between good and bad landscape solutions. There is no single, finite solution to any landscape design. The goal is only to achieve the best solution for you—your needs, your wants, and your property. Through your travels and your daily observance of your surroundings, you will begin to relate many aspects of other landscapes to those of your own garden. And as your awareness of landscaping evolves, you will be even more impressed and appreciative of good garden design. In landscaping, as in life, we continue to learn and to deepen our understanding of the nuances of nature and people season after season.

About the Authors

George and Brian Kay are a father-and-son team of landscape architects who specialize in residential landscaping. They operate George Kay & Associates, a landscape design and construction firm founded in 1979 with an office and two nurseries in the Chicago suburbs. Their work is primarily seen in the Chicago metropolitan area, as well as in clients' vacation homes in Colorado, Wisconsin, and Indiana. Their landscape design work has appeared in *Better Homes and Gardens*.

George Kay is an award-winning landscape designer. Before starting his own business, he worked for D. Hill Nursery in Dundee, Illinois, for twenty-two years. There he developed and managed two garden centers and the landscape department. He is the author of *Landscape Plans*, a guidebook to residential landscaping. He is coauthor, with Kaneji Domoto, of *Bonsai and the Japanese Garden*, published by Countryside Books. The American Association of Nurserymen has recognized his work—including the Union Oil Facility in Chicago and the Lions Clubs

International Headquarters in Oak Brook, Illinois—with Presidential Awards presented by then-First Ladies Ladybird Johnson and Pat Nixon.

Brian Kay is a registered landscape architect. His experience includes golf course construction and architecture for Wadsworth Golf Construction Company and Packard Inc. Prior to joining George Kay & Associates, he worked as a landscape architect, land planner, and has held a variety of jobs in the landscape and nursery businesses that he calls "learning experiences." These include D. Hill Nursery in Dundee, Illinois; Tanner Associates in Fort Myers, Florida; Post, Buckley, Schuh & Jernigan (PBS&J) in Orlando, Florida; and Glyman Design Group in Boca Raton, Florida, and Dallas.

Jennifer Derryberry Mann is a freelance writer and editor based in Minneapolis. She has edited magazines for the floriculture and agriculture industries, and she helps horticulture businesses develop content for their Web sites and marketing materials. As a freelance writer, Jennifer also covers the topics of health and fitness, spirituality and well being, sustainability, and business. Her writing has appeared in publications including *Fit Pregnancy*, *Pregnancy*, *Modern Bride Connection*, *Spirituality & Health*, *Corporate EVENT*, and *Sales & Marketing Management*.

Index

A

Access to back garden, 49–50
Angell house, 54–56
Annuals, 52–53
Arbors, 100
Architectural style
    front walk and, 28
    matching landscape style to, 9–10
Art pieces, 48, 63, 65

B

Back garden, 43–65
    access to, 49–50
    art pieces in, 48, 63, 65
    comfort in, 79–81
    coziness in, 85
    deck in, 44, 62, 63
    exterior design for, 47
    fencing in, 50
    flowers in, 52–53
    garden in, 79–80
    gathering space in, 79–80
    gazebo in, 45
    for Greek Revival home, 74
    hard surfaces in, 85–86
    for historical home, 57–59
    information for landscape
        professionals on, 93, 94
    landscape lighting for, 50
    natural appeal in, 85–87

outdoor kitchen in, 45–46

outdoor rooms in, 60–61

  furnishings for, 47–48

party space in, 54–56

patio in, 44–45, 62, 63

pergolas in, 50

personal style of, 48

plants for, 49, 51–53, 59, 63, 80–81

play space in, 46

pond in, 53

pool/spa in, 46–47

privacy in, 50, 55, 85

retaining wall in, 58, 85–86

room to grow in, 60–61

screening in, 50

trees in, 52

trellises in, 50

vantage point in, 53

walk in, 80, 87

as wooded retreat, 62–65

Benches, 97–98

Bilton house, 82–87

Boulder walls, 55

Brick pavers for front walk, 28

Bubble diagram, 69, 70

Builder's walk, 27

Bulbs, 52–53

C

Cape Cod–style home, 10

  fencing for, 36–37

  front walk for, 37

  plantings for, 37–38

Cattle walk, 28

Circular drive, 26

Classic farmhouse, 9

Clay brick pavers, 28

Comfortable design, 76–81

back garden in, 79–81

front garden in, 76–79

Common lilac, 7

Composition of plants, 5–6

Concrete for front walk, 28

Container gardens, 29

Courtyards, 78

Coziness in back garden, 85

Curb appeal, 34–35, 71

Current functions, 20–21

D

Deciduous trees, 5

Decks, 44, 62, 63

Delcampo house, 76–81

Depth, 6–8

Development

  further, 71

  phased, 71

Drainage, 19–20

Driveway

  circular, 26

  front garden and, 31, 76–77, 82–83

  garage door and, 26–27

Dwarf lilac, 7

Dwarf plantings, 7

E

Entertaining, house for, 54–56

  boulder walk in, 55

  plants for, 54–55

  privacy and, 55

  transformation in, 56

Entrance, front, 77–78

Evergreens, 5

Expansion, room for, 60–61

Exterior design in back garden, 47

F

Fallingwater (Frank Lloyd Wright), 3
Fencing, 25–26
    for back garden, 50
    for front garden, 36–37
Flowering crabapple, 6
Flowers. *See also* Plants
    annuals, 52–53
    for back garden, 52–53
    perennial, 29, 52–53
Focal points, creating, 8
Focus on function, 4
Form follows function, xii
Foundation, settling around, 19
Fountains, 65
Freestanding walls, 102
Front garden, 23–41
    builder shortcuts and, 39–41
    Cape Cod style, 36–38
    comfortable design and, 76–79
    curb appeal, 34–35
    driveway and, 31, 76–77, 82–83
    driveway and garage door, 26–27
    entrance and, 77–78
    fencing and, 25–26, 36–37
    front porch for, 35
    front walk in, 31–32, 37, 39–40
    for Greek Revival home, 73–74
    hardscape in, 24–26
    information for landscape
        professionals on, 93, 94
    landscape planning, 24
    natural appeal in, 82–85
    outdoor rooms for, 35
    parking spaces and, 83
    plants in, 28–29, 32, 35, 37–38,
        78–80, 84–85
    retaining wall in, 25, 35, 41, 83–84

walks in, 27–28, 34, 77
    as welcome retreat, 31–33
Front porch, 35
Front walk, 27–28
    in front garden, 31–32, 37, 39–40
    materials for, 28
    placement of, 28
    size of, 28
    views in, 30
Function, focusing on, 4
Functional landscape, designing, 4–5
Furnishings for outdoor room, 47–48
Further development, 71

G

Garden
    art in, 10–11
    design of, xi–xii
    Japanese-style, 98
Garden envy, xi
Garden structures, 93–103
    freestanding wall, 102
    gate, 98–99
    lattice or trellis, 100
    lawn ornament, 103
    pergola or arbor, 100
    pool or pond, 103
    statuary, 101–102
Gates
    garden, 98–99
    as garden structures, 98–99
Gathering spaces, 79–80
Gazebo in back garden, 45
Golitz house, 62–65
Grading, 24–25, 83
Grass, 29
Greek Revival home, 9, 72–75
    back garden for, 74

front garden for, 73–74

harmony in, 75

Groundcover, 29, 32

H

Hard edges, softening, 5

Hardscape, 4–5, 24–26

grading, 24–25

Hard surfaces in back garden, 85–86

Harmony, 67–87

Herbaceous plantings, 28–29

Historical home

back garden in, 57–59

outdoor rooms for, 60–61

planning in, 59–60

plants for, 59, 61

private space in, 60

public space in, 60

retaining wall for, 58

view in, 57

I

Intangible rewards, 71

J

Japanese-style garden, 98

Jefferson, Thomas, Monticello, 3

K

Kemp house, 60–61

Kitchen, outdoor, 45–46

Krupke house, 39–41

L

Landscape, 15–21

imagining dream, 67–69

lighting for, 50

matching to architectural style, 9–10

Landscape architects, 71, 92

Landscape design

composition of plants, 6–7

avoiding mistakes, 13

being good neighbor, 10–11

creating focal points and enhancing views, 8

maintaining privacy, 11–12

matching style to your house's architectural style, 9–10

proportion and adding depth, 6–8

principles of, 3–13

focus on function, 4

hardscape, 4–5

Landscape designers, 92

Landscape professionals, 91–95

information about property for, 93–95

working with, 93

Lattice as garden structures, 100

Lawn ornaments, 103

Lighting for back garden, 50

M

Master plan, 67–71

budget for improvements, 71

creating, 69–71

planning for future, 71

Materials in front walk, 28

Mediterranean style, 9

Michelangelo, Sistine Chapel, 3

Migley house, 57–59

Mistakes, avoiding, 13

Monticello (Thomas Jefferson), 3

Multiple-stemmed trees, 52

Mustache plantings, xii, 8

N

Natural appeal, 82–87
  back garden in, 85–87
  front garden in, 82–85
Neighbor, being good, 10–11

O

Objectivity, 15
Off-site views, 16
Orientation, 18
Outdoor kitchen, 45–46
Outdoor rooms
  in back garden, 60–61
  in front garden, 35
  furnishings for, 47–48

P

Parking spaces, 83
Parkway trees, 52
Paths in back garden, 49–50
Patio in back garden, 44–45, 47, 62, 63
Perennial flowers, 29, 52–53
Pergolas, 50, 100
Personal style in back garden, 48
Phased development, 71
Place for front walk, 28
Plants. *See also* Flowers
  in back garden, 49, 51–53, 59, 63,
    80–81
  composition of, 5–6
  in front garden, 28–29, 32, 35,
    37–38, 78–79, 78–80, 84–85
  herbaceous, 28–29
Plat of survey, 16–18
Play space in back garden, 46

Ponds
  in back garden, 53
  as garden structures, 103
Pools/spas, 46–47
  in back garden, 46–47
  as garden structures, 103
Powers house, 34–35
Privacy
  in back garden, 50, 55, 85
  maintaining, 10–12
  screening for, 16
Proportion, 6–8

R

Recirculation pump, 19
Referral, 92
Retaining wall, 25
  in back garden, 58, 85–86
  in front garden, 35, 41, 83–84

S

Schiffer house, 31–33
Schulenburg house, 36–38, 72–75
Screening for back garden, 50
Shade trees, 5, 29
Side-loading garages, 27
Single-stem trees, 52
Sistine Chapel (Michelangelo), 3
Size of front walk, 28
Spacing of plants, 8
Statuary
  in back garden, 48
  as garden structures, 101–102
Stock, taking, 21
Sump pump, 19

T

Trees
    in back garden, 52
    deciduous, 5
    evergreen, 5
    multiple-stemmed, 52
    parkway, 52
    shade, 5, 29
    single-stem, 52

Trellis
    in back garden, 50
    as garden structure, 100

V

Vantage point in back garden, 53
Victorian style, 9

Views
    creating beautiful, 30
    enhancing, 8
    improving, 30
    off-site, 16

W

Walks
    in back garden, 49–50, 80, 87
    in front garden, 34, 77
Welcoming home, 31–33
Wooded retreat, 62–65
Woody plantings, 28–29
Wright, Frank Lloyd, Fallingwater, 3